P9-DGE-333

COOK THE PERFECT...

MARCUS WAREING

WITH JENI WRIGHT

COOK THE PERFECT...

LONDON NEW YORK MUNICH MELBOURNE DELHI

For my family—Jane, Jake, and Archie—with love from Marcus

Project Editor Norma MacMillan
Project Art Editors and Designers Smith & Gilmour London
Photographer David Loftus
Americanization Editor Christy Lusiak
US Recipe Consultant Rick Rodgers
Senior Editor Dawn Henderson
Senior Art Editor Susan Downing
DTP Designer Traci Salter
Production Controller Luca Frassinetti

First American Edition, 2007

**Published in the United States by
DK Publishing, 375 Hudson Street
New York, New York 10014**

07 08 09 10 11   10 9 8 7 6 5 4 3 2 1

BD302—April 2007

Published in Great Britain by Dorling Kindersley Ltd.

**A Cataloging-in-Publication record for this book is available from the
Library of Congress.**

ISBN 978-0-7566-2624-2

**DK books are available at special discounts for bulk purchases for
sales promotions, premiums, fund-raising, or educational use. For
details, contact: DK Publishing Special Markets, 375 Hudson Street,
New York, NY 10014 or SpecialSales@dk.com**

**Color reproduction by MDP, UK
Printed and bound by Hung Hing, China**

**Discover more at
www.dk.com**

CONTENTS

MY CHARTER FOR SUCCESSFUL COOKING

After all the years I've been cooking, it's struck me how much more there is to know about a recipe than what's written down. Professionals have a level of understanding that most readers don't, and very few recipe books provide it. This led me to consider how good it would be to dig really deep into my recipes and strip them back to the basics, pinpointing the hows and whys, and even the pitfalls, while sharing the key to perfection for every one of them. So this is what I've done in this book, and I'm sure it will give you the confidence to tackle any dish you choose, even if you've never cooked it before. But before you start, please read my 10-point charter for success, opposite. In my restaurants and at home, I always follow these same, simple rules. If you follow them too, I guarantee you'll not only enjoy cooking, but you'll get perfect results every time.

1

Plan ahead before you start cooking
Read the recipe from start to finish, making sure you understand both the ingredients and the method. If you can do this the day before, so much the better.

2

Keep a good pantry
Staple items in your kitchen cupboards and refrigerator will provide the basis for good meals, and save you time.

3

Make a shopping list
Check to see what you have, and write down what you are missing.

4

Shop for fresh ingredients on the day
Buy only as much as you need, and take time to find the best.

5

Read the recipe again
Sit down, take your time, and make a plan of action, allowing adequate time for each step.

6

Dress the part
Put your apron on and clear your working area, then start assembling all the ingredients and equipment.

7

Be prepared
Before starting to cook, measure ingredients and complete any preparation steps like peeling, slicing, and chopping.

8

Tidy and clean as you go
Keep your work area clear of clutter at all times, from starting the recipe to serving the dish.

9

Re-organize
If things aren't going to plan, stop and take stock of the situation, then re-organize before carrying on.

10

Enjoy cooking
Last but not least, relax and be confident. The food will taste all the better for it.

SOUPS

CHINESE NOODLE SOUP

When I'm in a big city, wherever it is in the world, I always go to Chinatown. Seeing Chinese people there eating noodle soup tells me it must be good, and I just love the powerful flavor of the broth with the simple vegetables and noodles. When I recreate noodle soup at home and want to make it into a more substantial meal, I add strips of cooked chicken, duck, or beef at the end.

SERVES 4
6 cups Beef Stock (opposite)
4 celery ribs, strings removed and very finely sliced
1 carrot, peeled and pared into ribbons with a vegetable peeler, then cut into julienne
1 leek (white part only), very finely sliced
6 scallions, very finely sliced
4oz (100g) dried Chinese egg noodles (medium thickness)
sea salt and freshly milled black pepper

TO SERVE
soy sauce
Asian dark sesame oil

Bring the beef stock to a boil over high heat, then simmer for 15–20 minutes until reduced to about half its original volume. As the volume decreases, the flavor increases.

While the stock is simmering, bring a pan of salted water to a boil over high heat. Add the celery, carrot, leek, and scallions, bring back to a boil, and blanch for 2 minutes. Lift out with a slotted spoon, transfer to a colander, and rinse under cold water.

Plunge the noodles into the vegetable blanching water and bring back to a boil, stirring to separate the strands. Simmer for 4 minutes, then drain.

Divide the vegetables and noodles among warmed bowls. Check and correct the seasoning of the stock, then ladle into the bowls on top of the vegetables and noodles. Serve immediately, with soy sauce and sesame oil for seasoning at the table.

BEEF STOCK

MAKES ABOUT 6 CUPS
about 6¹/₂lb (3kg) beef bones,
   chopped (ask your butcher
   to do this)
vegetable oil, for frying
3 carrots, peeled and halved
   crosswise
2 onions, quartered lengthwise
3 whole leeks, cut crosswise
   into 1¹/₄in (3cm) lengths
¹/₂ bulb garlic (cut crosswise)
3 celery ribs, halved crosswise
3 sprigs of fresh or dried thyme
1 bay leaf
3 tbsp tomato paste

Preheat the oven to 425°F (220°C). Roast the bones in a very large, heavy roasting pan for about 30 minutes until dark golden brown, turning them every 10 minutes or so. Lift the bones out and let the excess fat drain off, then put them in a very large, heavy pan. Pour in cold water to cover (about 4¹/₂ quarts/4.5 liters) and bring to a boil.

Meanwhile, heat 4 tbsp oil in a large, heavy pan and fry the carrots over high heat until dark golden brown all over. Remove with a slotted spoon and drain in a colander. Repeat with the onions, then the leeks and garlic, and finally the celery, adding more oil as needed. Return all the vegetables to the pan and stir in the thyme, bay leaf, and tomato paste. Cook for about 5 minutes, then drain in a colander.

When the water begins to boil, skim and then add the vegetables. Bring back to a boil and skim again, then turn the heat down to very low. Cook very gently for 4–6 hours, uncovered, skimming regularly.

Ladle into a colander set over a bowl, then pass the strained stock through a cheesecloth-lined sieve into a clean pan. Boil until reduced to about 6 cups. Use immediately, or cool quickly and refrigerate in a covered container; remove any surface fat before using.

KEY TO PERFECTION
Simple soups like this one rely on their stock for flavor and body, so you must get the stock right.

After roasting the bones, put them in a large sieve or colander set over a pan or bowl, and leave next to the stove for 10 minutes. This will drain off the fat, so you will have less skimming to do later and the stock will not be greasy.

During the long cooking time, keep the heat very low so the stock barely murmurs. Don't let the stock boil or fat will come out of the bones into the stock, and the vegetables will break down and make the stock cloudy.

Fat and scum make stock greasy and cloudy, so frequent skimming during simmering is essential. Use a ladle, taking care to keep it only just below the surface of the liquid.

"For a fabulous dinner party main course, serve each portion topped with a steamed fillet of cod or sea bass."

FRENCH ONION SOUP

One of the classics of French cooking, this is one of the first dishes I made when I was training at The Savoy hotel in London. My recipe has all the hallmarks of a perfect *soupe à l'oignon* — tender onions, a rich, wine-laced broth, and a crown of golden cheese croûtes.

SERVES 4
5 white onions, peeled
3 tbsp vegetable oil
4 tbsp (½ stick) unsalted
   butter, diced
2 large sprigs of fresh thyme
5 garlic cloves, finely chopped
2 cups red wine, either Burgundy
   or Bordeaux
4 cups hot Beef Stock (page 11)
sea salt and freshly milled
   black pepper

TO FINISH
about 2 tbsp finely chopped
   fresh chervil or parsley
Cheese Croûtes (below)

Halve the onions lengthwise, place cut side down, and cut across into ¼in (5mm) thick slices. In a large, heavy pan, heat the oil and butter until foaming. Add the onions, thyme, and seasoning, and cook over low to medium heat for a few minutes before stirring in the garlic. Cover and cook gently for 15–20 minutes, stirring frequently.

Pour in the wine, increase the heat to high, and boil rapidly for about 10 minutes until the wine has all but disappeared. Pour in the stock and bring to a boil, then skim off any fat or scum with a ladle. Simmer gently, uncovered, for 45 minutes to 1 hour, skimming occasionally.

To finish, check and correct the seasoning of the soup, then ladle into warmed bowls, packing them with plenty of onions. Sprinkle with chervil and top with the croûtes.

CHEESE CROÛTES

MAKES 16
16 thin slices of baguette
olive oil, for drizzling
4oz (100g) Gruyère or Cheddar
   cheese, grated

Preheat the oven to 425°F (220°C). Put the baguette slices on an oiled baking sheet and drizzle with olive oil. Bake for 3–5 minutes until they are crisp and golden.

Turn the slices over and bake for another 3–5 minutes. Top with the grated cheese. Return to the oven (or pop under the broiler) and bake for 1–2 minutes until melted.

"I always use firm, white onions for this soup. They have more flavor than large brown-skinned ones, which can be watery."

KEY TO PERFECTION

You need to get the consistency and color of the onions right before adding the stock. At first they must be cooked until soft, but they must not be browned or the soup will taste bitter. Then they need to be saturated with wine to give the soup color, body, and flavor.

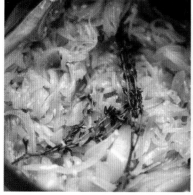

At the end of boiling with the wine, the softened onions will become a deep burgundy red and almost dry. When you hear them start to sizzle on the bottom of the pan, it's time to take them off the heat.

Fry the onions gently at the beginning so they soften with only a very light coloring. Covering the pan helps, as the water from inside the lid drips onto them and keeps them moist.

PUMPKIN SOUP

Gordon Ramsay, who is now an international television star, taught me how to make this when we were working together in the early 90s. Just a few ingredients are needed to make a silky smooth soup.

SERVES 6
3lb (1.4kg) ripe pumpkin
7 tbsp (½ stick plus 3 tbsp)
   unsalted butter
5½ cups hot Chicken
   Stock (below)
4oz (100g) fresh Parmesan
   cheese, grated
3–4 tbsp heavy cream
sea salt and freshly milled
   black pepper

TO SERVE
extra-virgin olive oil
shavings of fresh Parmesan
   cheese

Cut the pumpkin into chunks and scrape out the seeds, then peel off the tough skin. Slice the pumpkin flesh thinly.

Heat the butter in a large, heavy saucepan over medium-high heat until it foams and turns nut brown. Add the pumpkin, sprinkle with salt, and stir well, then turn the heat down to low. Cover and cook gently for 15 minutes, shaking the pan from time to time.

Pour in the hot stock, increase the heat to high, and bring to a boil. Add the Parmesan and stir in, then turn the heat down to a gentle simmer. Cook uncovered for 15 minutes, stirring occasionally so the Parmesan doesn't stick on the bottom of the pan.

Purée the soup in a blender, working in batches, then strain the purée through a fine sieve into a clean pot. Whisk in the cream. Reheat the soup gently, then taste and correct the seasoning if necessary.

Ladle the soup into warmed bowls, drizzle with some olive oil, and top with Parmesan shavings. Serve immediately.

CHICKEN STOCK

MAKES ABOUT 5½ CUPS
1 chicken, preferably organic,
   weighing about 3½lb (1.5kg)
2 onions, cut into ¾in (2cm)
   pieces
1 leek (both green and
   white parts), cut into
   ¾in (2cm) pieces
3 celery ribs, cut into
   ¾in (2cm) pieces
½ bulb garlic (cut crosswise)
1 sprig of fresh or dried thyme
2 bay leaves
sea salt

Cut the breast meat off the rib cage of the chicken and reserve the boneless breasts for another use. Chop the rest of the chicken in half and rinse in cold water, then put in a large, heavy pot and cover with cold water. Bring to a boil over high heat, skimming off the scum with a ladle.

When the stock is clear of scum, add the onions, leek, celery, garlic, thyme, and bay leaves, and bring back to a boil. Skim again, turn the heat down to a very gentle simmer, and cook uncovered for 2½ hours, skimming regularly. Toward the end of cooking, taste and add salt. You should add the salt a little at a time until you get the correct seasoning.

Strain the stock through a fine sieve into a clean pot or bowl, pressing down on the vegetables and bones with a ladle to get all the liquid from them. Use the stock immediately, or cool quickly and refrigerate in a covered container, then remove any surface fat before using.

KEY TO PERFECTION

For a velvety texture, the pumpkin must be thoroughly cooked at each stage or it won't purée smoothly in the blender.

Put the lid on the saucepan while the pumpkin is cooking in the butter at the beginning. This will make the pumpkin sweat so that moisture will drip from inside the lid into the pan.

When the pumpkin has had a full 15 minutes gently sweating in butter, it will break up and release its juices. This is the cue for adding the stock.

At the end of simmering in the stock, you will know the pumpkin is ready for blending when it's as soft as butter.

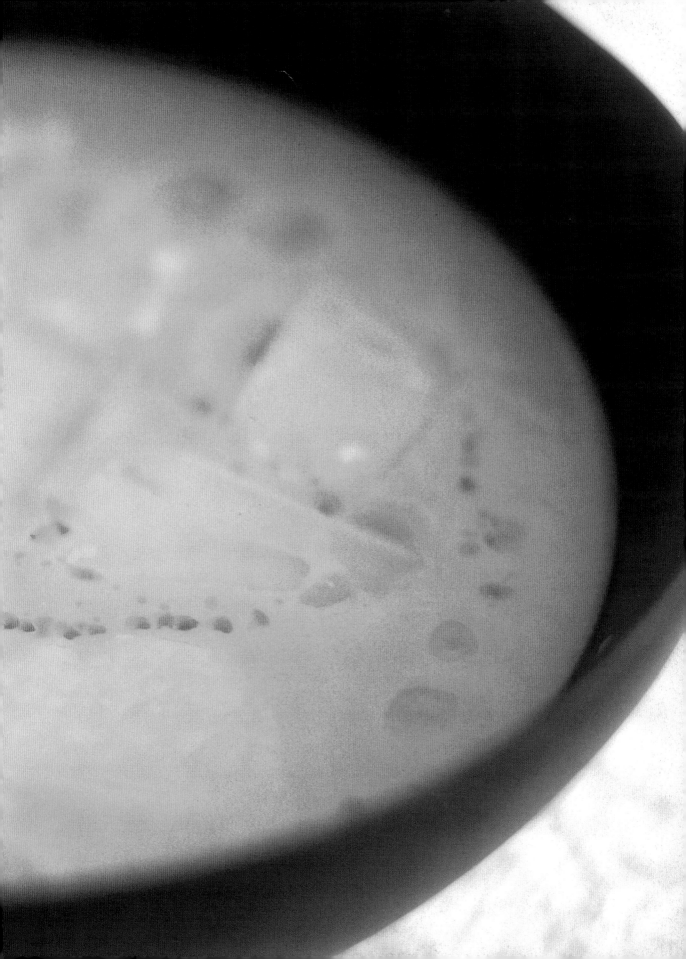

CREAMY MUSHROOM SOUP

The intense mushroom flavor of this soup is its *raison d'être*, and I don't try to camouflage it. The cream and butter make it very rich and silky smooth without detracting from the earthy taste.

SERVES 4–6
1¾lb (750g) full-flavored
   mushrooms
½ cup olive oil
3 large shallots, finely sliced
2 garlic cloves, finely chopped
juice of ½ lemon
4 cups hot Chicken Stock
   (page 16)
1 cup heavy cream
7 tbsp (½ stick plus 3 tbsp)
   unsalted butter, diced
sea salt and freshly milled
   white pepper

FOR THE SHALLOT
AND HERB CREAM
⅓ cup heavy cream
1–2 small shallots, finely diced
1 sprig each of fresh chervil,
   tarragon, and cilantro,
   finely chopped
a few stems of fresh chives,
   finely snipped

Wipe the mushrooms clean with a damp cloth, then slice them thinly. Heat the oil in a large, heavy saucepan. Add the shallots and cook over low heat for a few minutes until softened, then stir in the garlic and soften for a minute or two longer. Add the mushrooms and sprinkle with a little salt. Increase the heat to get the mushrooms cooking, then toss and stir to mix them with the shallots and garlic. Cover and cook gently for 5–8 minutes, stirring occasionally.

Squeeze in the lemon juice and reduce a little, then pour in the stock and stir well. Increase the heat to high and bring to a boil. Turn the heat down and simmer uncovered for 10 minutes, stirring occasionally, until the mushrooms are really soft.

Purée the soup in a blender in batches, adding the cream while the machine is running. Keep blending until smooth.

Make the shallot and herb cream by lightly whipping the cream, then adding the shallots, herbs, and seasoning. Fold the ingredients together until well combined.

To finish, pour the soup into a clean pan and heat through, whisking in the diced butter until melted. Taste for seasoning, then ladle into warmed bowls and top with the shallot and herb cream.

"Only use full-flavored mushrooms, such as cremini, for this soup, and don't worry if they're starting to shrivel. Older mushrooms contain less water than very fresh mushrooms, so their flavor is more concentrated."

KEY TO PERFECTION

To get the intense mushroom flavor that is the keynote of this soup,
you must cook the mushrooms until they reduce down to a fraction
of their original size. This is the way to concentrate their flavor.

Pour the pile of raw mushrooms over
the shallot and garlic mix. Don't
worry if there seems to be too many
mushrooms for the pan—they will
start to shrink once cooking begins.

Stir the mushrooms several times
during cooking, to make sure they
cook evenly. Each time you stir
you'll notice how they've shrunk
down in the pan.

After simmering in stock, the mushrooms
will have reduced down to a dark, juicy
mass that covers the bottom of the pan.

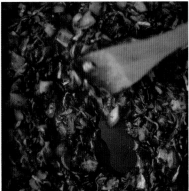
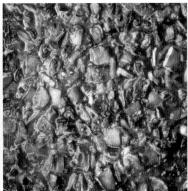

CUCUMBER AND YOGURT GAZPACHO

There is no one single recipe for gazpacho, the Spanish culinary icon, and it always amazes me how much it varies from one place to another. My version includes horseradish and dill, two ingredients that you might not expect to see in a gazpacho, and omits the tomato.

SERVES 6–8

3 unwaxed English cucumbers, finely sliced (including the skin)
1/4 large bunch of fresh dill, chopped with the stalks
2 tbsp bottled horseradish
3 cups chilled Vegetable Nage (below)
1 1/4 cups plain Greek yogurt
sea salt and freshly milled white pepper

TO SERVE

extra-virgin olive oil
very thin slices of focaccia bread, lightly toasted

Mix the cucumbers and dill in a bowl. Whisk the horseradish into the nage, season with salt, and mix with the cucumber and dill. Cover and refrigerate overnight.

Purée the refrigerated ingredients in batches with the yogurt until smooth, adding a few twists of pepper. Transfer to a clean bowl. Place this in a larger bowl half filled with ice cubes and refrigerate for 2–3 hours until well chilled.

When ready to serve, check and correct the seasoning of the soup, then ladle into chilled bowls. Garnish with droplets of olive oil, and accompany with toasted focaccia.

VEGETABLE NAGE

This needs to be made the day before required.

MAKES 3 CUPS

1 leek, outside leaves discarded, cut into 1 1/4in (3cm) lengths
4 carrots, peeled and cut into 3/4in (2cm) lengths
2 white onions, each cut lengthwise into eighths
2 celery ribs, cut into 1 1/4in (3cm) lengths
3 garlic cloves, peeled and left whole
1 star anise
1/2 tsp coriander seeds
1/4 tsp white peppercorns
a handful of mixed fresh herbs, including parsley, basil, chives, and chervil
3 lemon wedges
1/2 cup dry white wine

Put all the vegetables and garlic into a large, heavy pot. Pour in about 4 cups cold water—enough to reach the same level as the vegetables—and bring to a boil over high heat. Skim off any froth, then turn the heat down to medium and simmer uncovered for exactly 8 minutes.

While the vegetables are simmering, crush the star anise with the coriander seeds and peppercorns in a mortar or under a heavy skillet.

As soon as the 8 minutes are up, add the crushed spices to the liquid along with the herbs and lemon wedges. Simmer uncovered for a further 2 minutes, then immediately take the pan off the heat and stir in the wine. Let cool completely.

Ladle the liquid and vegetables into a glass or plastic container, cover tightly, and refrigerate for 24 hours.

The next day, strain the liquid through a fine sieve. Discard the vegetables. Keep the nage covered in the refrigerator until ready to use.

KEY TO PERFECTION

For a delicate chilled soup, it is important to use the right liquid for the base flavor. Chicken or vegetable stock would be too strong, water too weak. Scented vegetable nage is the answer.

Spices, fresh herbs, and lemon wedges add their scent and flavor to the vegetables and liquid, but they should be heated for only 2 minutes or their freshness will be lost.

As soon as the nage is cold, decant it into a container and refrigerate it. Don't let it sit at room temperature or the vegetables will become slimy.

Use the finest sieve you have for straining this delicate stock. The liquid should come through crystal clear.

ALL IS NOT LOST

If you think the soup isn't cold enough when you are ready to serve, give it a chill boost by submerging a plastic bag of ice cubes in it for a few minutes.

PLAN AHEAD BEFORE YOU START COOKING

"Read the recipe from start to finish, making sure you understand both the ingredients and the method. If you can do this the day before, so much the better."

LEEK AND POTATO SOUP

This soup makes a perfect first course for a dinner party, because it looks elegant and its delicate flavor won't clash with anything that comes after it. In the summer I serve it chilled, when it can be called by its French name, *vichyssoise*.

SERVES 6

5 large leeks, about 2¼lb (1kg) in total

2 baking potatoes, such as russet or Burbank, about 14oz (400g) in total

10 tbsp (1¼ sticks) unsalted butter

1 white onion, finely sliced

3 garlic cloves, chopped

3 cups boiling hot Chicken Stock (page 16)

3–4 tbsp heavy cream

sea salt and freshly milled white pepper

TO SERVE

6 tbsp heavy cream

finely snipped fresh chives

Cut off and discard the roots of the leeks and the dark green tops, leaving behind some of the light green. You should be left with 1½–1¾lb (700–800g) leeks to use. Cut them in half lengthwise, then slice across into fine strips. Wash the strips well in cold water and drain. Peel the potatoes (you should have 10–12oz (300–350g) to use after peeling) and rinse briefly. Cut into wedges and slice finely. Don't wash the slices—the potato starch will help thicken the soup.

Heat 7 tbsp of the butter in a large, heavy saucepan over medium heat until foaming. Add the onion and garlic, and stir and cook without coloring for a couple of minutes until they start to soften. Add the leeks, season with salt, and stir well. Cover the pan tightly and cook over medium-high heat for 8 minutes, stirring occasionally.

Mix the potatoes in with the leeks, then stir in the boiling stock a ladleful at a time. Immediately bring back to a boil, then cover and cook for 8 minutes longer until both potatoes and leeks are tender.

Working in batches, purée the soup immediately in a blender until smooth, adding the cream and the remaining butter in small pieces while the machine is running. Now strain the soup through a sieve into a clean saucepan and reheat gently without boiling.

Taste and correct the seasoning if necessary, and serve topped with a swirl of cream and a sprinkling of chives.

"You need just enough potatoes to give body to the leeks without making the soup floury and bland. Don't go by the number of vegetables alone —a successful marriage of leeks and potatoes is also judged by weight."

KEY TO PERFECTION

The hallmark of a good leek and potato soup is its velvety smoothness. Cooking the leeks and potatoes together to the same degree of softness is the secret behind this. Undercooked leeks will be stringy, and no amount of blending and sieving will get rid of this.

It is important to slice the potatoes very thinly so they cook in half the time it takes the leeks to become soft. If the potatoes are added too early they will overcook and become grainy; if they're added too late, the leeks will overcook before the potatoes are done.

By the time you add the potatoes, the leeks will be half cooked. They should be glossy and bright green.

With the help of a small ladle, perfectly cooked leeks and potatoes will pass freely through the sieve after blending. A conical sieve called a *chinois* makes the job easy because it allows you to press and rotate the ladle against the inside to push the vegetables through.

ROASTED TOMATO SOUP

My boys love tomato soup, so I often make this at home. Served with crusty bread and cheese, it makes a complete meal, and it's so easy because it needs virtually no cooking. The great flavor comes from the combination of roasted fresh tomatoes and sun-dried tomatoes.

SERVES 4
2/3 cup olive oil
1/2 small white onion, roughly chopped
3 garlic cloves, sliced
2 1/4 lb (1 kg) over-ripe, full-flavored tomatoes
1 cup sun-dried tomatoes in oil
3 sprigs of fresh basil
3 sprigs of fresh cilantro
2 tbsp tomato paste
Worcestershire sauce, to taste
balsamic vinegar, to taste
2 cups hot Chicken Stock (page 16)
sea salt and freshly milled black pepper

TO SERVE
extra-virgin olive oil
fresh basil leaves

Preheat the oven to 475°F (240°C). Heat a large roasting pan in the oven for 3–4 minutes. Pour the oil into the hot pan, then add the onion, garlic, and the whole fresh tomatoes. Season and stir, then place in the oven to roast for 15 minutes.

Stir in the sun-dried tomatoes and their oil, and scatter the herbs over the top. Roast for 10 minutes longer, then mix in the tomato paste and roast for a final 5 minutes.

Pour the contents of the pan into a large bowl, add 2 tbsp each Worcestershire sauce and balsamic vinegar, and stir well. Cover the bowl with plastic wrap and let marinate for half an hour.

Purée the soup in batches in a blender until smooth, then pass through a fine sieve into a pot. Heat to a simmer, then pour in the stock and stir well. Taste and correct the seasoning, adding up to 4 tsp more Worcestershire sauce and 3 tsp more balsamic vinegar, if you like.

Serve hot, topping each bowl with a drizzle of olive oil, some basil leaves, and freshly milled black pepper.

"Tomatoes love Worcestershire sauce —just think of a Bloody Mary. Here I've used balsamic vinegar as well. These two strong seasonings complement one another, and hold their own against the intense tomato flavor."

KEY TO PERFECTION

For the intense, smoky flavor that sets this soup apart from any other tomato soup, the secret is in the way the tomatoes are cooked.

Roast the fresh tomatoes until they blister and burst. Don't worry if the sun-dried tomatoes are tinged with black. The skins are sieved out before serving, but the lovely smoky flavor will be left behind.

ALL IS NOT LOST

If you've been a little heavy handed with the seasonings and the soup tastes too powerful, you can whisk in a few small pieces of unsalted butter at the reheating stage. The butter will mellow the flavor, and take the edge off any sharpness.

RICH CHICKEN SOUP

This is a very special chicken soup. Cooking the chicken in homemade stock concentrates the flavor, then using the stock to make a velouté sauce gives the soup a wonderful creamy consistency without adding cream. Served with hot crusty bread, it makes a great lunch or supper.

SERVES 6

1 chicken, preferably organic, weighing 3¼lb (1.5kg)
5½ cups cold Chicken Stock (page 16)
2 large carrots, peeled and cut into ¾in (2cm) dice
1 yellow onion, cut into ¾in (2cm) dice
2 celery ribs, strings removed and cut into ¾in (2cm) dice
1 leek (white part only), cut into ¾in (2cm) dice
2 garlic cloves, minced
7 tbsp (½ stick plus 3 tbsp) unsalted butter
⅔ cup all-purpose flour
sea salt and freshly milled black pepper

TO SERVE

shavings of fresh Parmesan cheese
a small handful of finely shredded fresh flat-leaf parsley

Remove the string and any giblets from the chicken. Soak the bird in a bowl of cold water for 10 minutes, so there will be less scum on the surface of the stock.

Drain the chicken and put it in a large, heavy pot. Pour in the stock and about 2½ quarts (2.5 liters) cold water to cover the bird, then add a pinch of salt. Bring to a boil over high heat. Immediately skim off any fat and scum, then turn the heat down and simmer uncovered for 1¼ hours. Remove from the heat and let the chicken cool in the liquid.

Lift out the bird. Strain the stock, measure 7½ cups, and set aside; reserve the remaining stock for blanching the vegetables. Take the chicken meat from the bones, discarding the skin. Break the meat into large shreds with your fingers. Set aside.

Pour 2 cups of the unmeasured stock into a medium saucepan, add a pinch of salt, and bring to a boil. Add the carrots, onion, celery, and leek. Bring back to a boil and blanch for 2–3 minutes until just tender. Drain in a colander set in a bowl to catch the blanching liquid.

Mix the blanching liquid with the measured stock in a clean saucepan and bring to a boil. Add the garlic. Boil for 15–20 minutes to reduce to about 5½ cups. Turn the heat to low and keep the stock hot.

Make the velouté sauce in a large, heavy saucepan. Melt the butter over medium-high heat, sprinkle in the flour, and stir to make a roux. Gradually beat and whisk in the reduced hot stock. Bring to a boil and simmer, whisking, for about 5 minutes.

Add the shredded chicken and vegetables to the sauce and heat through gently. Taste and correct the seasoning, and add a little extra stock if the soup is too thick. Serve topped with shavings of Parmesan, shredded parsley, and freshly milled pepper.

KEY TO PERFECTION

The best chicken soups have a silky consistency, which comes from making a smooth velouté sauce with the stock—the French word *velouté* means velvety.

 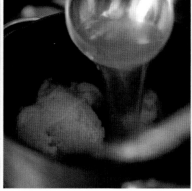 

Cook the butter and flour, stirring constantly with a wooden spoon, for 4–5 minutes until the mix becomes a light golden paste or roux. Don't skimp on the time—the flour must be thoroughly cooked or it will taste raw in the finished soup.

Add the stock to the roux a ladleful at a time, beating vigorously to blend it in after each addition. Beat with the spoon at first, then change to a whisk once the sauce becomes more liquid. This gradual addition of stock is the secret of a perfectly smooth sauce without lumps.

After simmering and whisking for 5 minutes, the flour will be thoroughly cooked and the sauce will have a velvety, pouring consistency.

FISH & SHELLFISH

SEARED TUNA

How you serve tuna is entirely up to you, but I prefer my tuna to be seared on the outside and rare in the center. When tuna is perfectly cooked, you don't need a lot of embellishments—just a drizzle of olive oil will suffice.

SERVES 2
2 tuna loin steaks, preferably yellowfin, cut 1in (2.5cm) thick and weighing 6–7oz (175–200g) each
olive oil
sea salt and cracked white pepper

Pat the fish with paper towels to remove any condensation. The fish should be completely dry before cooking.

Put a non-stick skillet over high heat, splash in enough oil to cover the bottom thinly, and heat until hot. To check the oil is hot enough, hold your hand about 3in (7cm) above the pan—you should feel the heat rising on your palm.

Sprinkle the fish on one side only with salt and pepper. Place seasoned side down in the hot oil and sprinkle the top with salt and pepper. Turn the heat down to medium-high and leave undisturbed for about 2 minutes.

Flip the fish over with a metal spatula, and cook undisturbed again for about 2 minutes. Remove the tuna to a cutting board and let rest for a few minutes.

Working across the grain with a very sharp knife, cut each steak into ¼in (5mm) thick slices. Serve sprinkled with salt and pepper, and drizzled with olive oil if you like.

KEY TO PERFECTION

For the best results, let your eyes do the timing as well as the clock. Recipes that give precise cooking times will often disappoint because they can't know the exact degree of heat you use, nor the type of pan or precise thickness of the steak.

On the first side, watch the color of the fish gradually change from the bottom of the steak until just below the halfway mark.

After flipping the fish, watch closely until the color changes to just below the halfway mark again. There should be a thin stripe of uncooked tuna running through the center.

ALL IS NOT LOST

If you don't have a non-stick pan, or the one you have has seen better days, you may find that the tuna sticks when the time comes to turn it over. Don't panic. Turn the heat up to high and leave the fish undisturbed for another minute or two until it gets well colored on the bottom and cooked up to the top edge. Then baste it with the hot oil from the pan to color the top. The underside will be crisp and dry, and the tuna will come away easily from the pan. The fish will be medium rather than rare, but it will look good—and it will be all in one piece.

"The thickness of the fish is important. If it's cut too thin the steak will overcook and be dry, but if it's too thick you'll find it difficult to get the center right without overcooking the outside. Always buy tuna from the fishmonger so you can get it cut to the exact thickness you want."

PAN-FRIED SCALLOPS

The French call scallops *Saint Jacques*, which goes back to medieval times when pilgrims traveling to Santiago de Compostela sustained themselves on scallops, and wore the shells as talismans. This way of cooking them brings out their natural sweetness.

SERVES 2
6 large fresh sea scallops,
    preferably diver
1 tsp mild curry powder
1 tsp fine sea salt
olive oil
Lentils with Herbs
    (page 142), to serve

Rinse the scallops in cold water and drain well. Lay them flat on one half of a cloth draped over a small baking sheet and cover with the other half of the cloth. Let dry in the refrigerator overnight.

Mix the curry powder and salt together, sprinkle over a plate, and leave overnight (the mix needs to dry out or the salt might make the scallops damp).

When you're ready to cook, put a non-stick skillet over medium-high heat. Splash in enough olive oil to cover the bottom of the pan thinly and heat until very hot.

Cut the scallops in half. Sprinkle half of the pieces with curry salt, then fry for about 20 seconds on each side. Drain on paper towels while cooking the rest of the scallops in the same way. Serve immediately, with the lentils.

"The drier the scallops are, the better—leaving them to dry out in the refrigerator overnight really helps with the cooking. This is especially beneficial if you're using dredged scallops (as compared to hand-collected diver scallops), most of which are very watery because they have been frozen and then defrosted."

KEY TO PERFECTION

The scallops must not be overcooked. To be sure they cook quickly and evenly, they should all be the same size, and each one should be in the hot frying pan for the same amount of time.

Stand each scallop up, holding it between your forefinger and thumb. Squeeze until you feel the flesh firm up, then make a clean slice through the center with a very sharp knife. You will now have 12 pieces that are similar in thickness.

Wait 10 seconds after putting the last one in, then sprinkle each scallop with curry salt and turn it over, starting with the one that went into the pan first and working clockwise. By the time you get to the last scallop, the first one will be ready to be removed.

Put 6 pieces of scallop on the fingertips, thumb, and heel of one hand, and sprinkle them with curry salt. Starting with the one on the heel of your hand, and working from 12 o'clock in a clockwise direction, put them seasoned side down in the hot frying pan in a semi-circle.

PAN-GRILLED SALMON

Fish that is pan-grilled correctly should have two textures—a crust on the outside and an undercooked center that is beautifully moist and soft. This gives you the best of both worlds, and is cooked exactly how I like it.

SERVES 4

4 center-cut (thick) salmon fillet
   portions, without skin,
   weighing about 7oz
   (200g) each
olive oil, for drizzling
sea salt and freshly milled
   black pepper
Bittersweet Greens Salad
   (page 114), to serve

Neaten each piece of salmon by trimming off any ragged edges. Pat the fish dry with paper towels.

Put a dry ridged grill pan over high heat until it is very hot. Drizzle the top (presentation) side of each fillet with olive oil and sprinkle with salt and pepper.

Turn the heat down to medium-high and put the salmon in the pan, laying it diagonally across the ridges with its presentation side down. Cook for 1½ minutes until seared underneath, then rotate the pieces in the opposite direction and cook for another 1½ minutes. Now turn the pieces over and cook for 3 minutes longer.

To serve, divide the salad among four plates, reserving a little of the dressing. Put the salmon on top of the salad, sprinkle with pepper, and drizzle the reserved dressing over the fish.

KEY TO PERFECTION

To get distinct chargrilled lines on fish so that it looks barbecued, you must let the fish sit still while it's cooking. Don't be tempted to shake the pan or move the fish, or you won't get an imprint of charred lines. Shaking the pan will also slow down the cooking, and moving or prodding the fish will release juices and make the fish watery—all the more reason not to do it.

After cooking for 3 minutes, first searing the fish in one direction and then the other, turn the pieces over to reveal the diamond pattern on the presentation side. Continue cooking for another 3 minutes without moving the fish—there is no need for a charred pattern on the skinned side of the fish as it will not be seen.

PAN-FRIED SEA BASS

I've learned that the simpler you prepare most fish, the better. I like to pan-fry sea bass fillets for a quick supper at home with my wife after the boys have gone to bed. The fish goes well with lots of things— a mixed leaf or endive salad, pasta or rice, or new potatoes tossed with chopped fresh mint and butter.

SERVES 4

1 whole sea bass, weighing
    2¹/₂–3lb (1.1–1.35kg), scaled,
    cleaned, and cut into 2 long
    fillets (ask the fishmonger
    to do this—you should
    end up with fillets weighing
    about 300g/10oz each)
olive oil
sea salt and freshly milled
    white pepper

Check for tiny pin bones in the flesh side of the fish and pull them out with pliers. Turn the fish over and score the skin, then cut each fillet in half crosswise to make four portions altogether. Season the scored skin with a little salt and pepper.

Put a large, non-stick skillet over high heat, splash in enough oil to cover the bottom thinly, and heat until hot.

Lower the heat to medium-high, put in the fish skin side down, and cook undisturbed for 4 minutes until the skin is crisp and golden. Don't shake the pan or move the fillets as this will cause moisture to come out of the fish—then the skin will stick to the pan and tear. If the pan gets too hot, draw it to the side of the heat and pour in a little cold oil to cool it down, then return it to the heat.

Turn the fish over and cook undisturbed for 2 minutes on the second side, basting with the hot oil so that it runs into the crevices in the skin.

To serve, place the sea bass skin side up on four plates and drizzle with the pan juices. Dust with white pepper if you like.

KEY TO PERFECTION

The skin of sea bass must be scored so the fish will stay flat during cooking. If the fish isn't flat, it won't cook evenly, and you won't be able to tell if it's done or not.

At the end of the cooking time, turn each piece of fish over onto its skin side again. Push down on the fish with your fingertips and hold them there for 10–15 seconds. The fish is ready when it feels firm, not spongy, and it should be removed from the hot pan immediately.

With a very sharp, large knife and a sawing action, cut diagonal slashes through the skin of each fillet. Make the score lines close together, and cut right through the skin just into the fish.

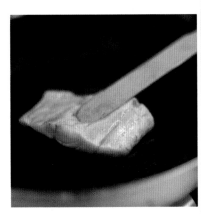

ALL IS NOT LOST

If you haven't scored the skin properly, or you've forgotten to score it at all, the fish will curl at the edges as soon as it goes in the pan, and then it won't cook evenly. Quickly press it hard with a spatula to force it down flat. You'll find it quite powerful and strong, so you'll need to use some force.

NEW ENGLAND CLAM CHOWDER

When I worked at a luxury resort in upstate New York, we served a chowder like this in a large tureen on the terrace at lunchtime—the guests helped themselves and ate it while enjoying the view of the beautiful Adirondack Mountains.

SERVES 4

3¼lb (1.5kg) fresh littleneck clams
10 tbsp (1¼ sticks) unsalted butter
¼ cup all-purpose flour
1 cup dry white wine
3 cups hot Fish Stock (opposite)
1 cup fresh corn kernels, or drained and rinsed canned corn
1 yellow onion, cut into ½in (1cm) dice
1 leek (white part only), cut into ½in (1cm) dice
2 garlic cloves, finely chopped
1 large baking potato, about 7oz (200g), peeled and cut into ½in (1cm) dice
⅔ cup heavy cream
a handful of fresh parsley (curly or flat-leaf), roughly chopped
sea salt and freshly milled white pepper

Clean the clams by soaking them in cold water for at least 20 minutes, or up to an hour.

Meanwhile, make a beurre manié (butter and flour *liaison*). Soften 4 tbsp of the butter and mix in the flour to make a thick paste. Keep in the refrigerator until ready to use.

Drain the clams in a colander and rinse under cold water to check there's no sand left in the shells. Discard any clams that are open or that do not close when tapped sharply on the countertop. Heat a wide saucepan over high heat until hot, add the clams and wine, and cover the pan tightly. Give the pan a shake, then take off the lid—some or all of the clams will be open. Remove the open ones with a slotted spoon and set aside. Put the lid on again, and continue until all the clams are out of the pan. (Discard any that stay closed.)

When the clams are cool enough to handle, remove them from their shells, reserving some in shells for garnishing. Pour the cooking liquid slowly through a fine sieve into a clean saucepan, leaving the sediment behind in the bottom of the first pan. Mix the hot fish stock with the cooking liquid and set aside.

If using fresh corn, blanch it in a small pan of salted boiling water for 1 minute, then drain and rinse under cold water.

Heat the remaining butter in a heavy saucepan over medium heat. Add the onion, leek, and garlic, and cook without coloring for a few minutes until they start to soften. Season with a little salt. Add the potato and cook for about 5 minutes until softened, then remove from the heat and stir in the shelled clams and corn. Set aside.

Bring the fish stock to a boil. Whisk in the beurre manié in small pieces, then boil and whisk until thickened. Stir in the cream and bring back to a boil, then add the clams and vegetables and heat through gently for a minute or two. Season lightly, and finish by adding the clams in their shells and the parsley. Serve hot.

FISH STOCK

MAKES ABOUT 6 CUPS
3¼lb (1.5kg) white fish bones with heads (from sole, bass, halibut, or snapper), gills and eyes removed
5 tbsp olive oil
1 yellow onion, cut into large dice
1 leek (white part only), cut into large dice
2 celery ribs, cut into large dice
1 bulb garlic, cut crosswise in half
10 coriander seeds
5 white peppercorns
1¼ cups dry white wine

Cut the fish bones into 2½in (6cm) pieces. Soak in cold water for 10 minutes, then drain in a colander.

Heat the oil in a large, heavy pot. Add the onion, leek, celery, garlic, and spices, stir, and cook over low heat for 5 minutes until the vegetables start to soften. Pour in the wine. Increase the heat, bring to a boil, and reduce for 2 minutes.

Add the fish bones and 6 cups cold water. Bring to a boil over high heat, then immediately turn down to a gentle simmer and shake the pan gently—most of the impurities will rise to the top. Skim off the scum with a ladle, then bring the stock back up to a moderate simmer. Cook for 20 minutes, skimming off any impurities as they appear.

Strain the stock through a colander set over a bowl. Discard the bones and vegetables, then strain the stock through a fine sieve into a clean pan or bowl. Use the stock immediately, or cool quickly and refrigerate in a covered container.

"Manila is a small clam that tends to be more tender than the larger types. You can use larger clams, such as cherrystones, but you will need to cook them for a few minutes longer initially and then cut the meat into small pieces. Cockles are an alternative to clams."

KEY TO PERFECTION

The liquid in a chowder should be like velvet, and there are two ways to achieve this. You should remove all the sand and grit from the clams before you start cooking, then use a butter and flour *liaison* (beurre manié) at the end to thicken the liquid and give it a smooth consistency. Classic recipes thicken the chowder once everything is in, but it's better to thicken the stock on its own so you don't crush the delicate potatoes and clams.

Whisk the beurre manié into the boiling liquid a teaspoon at a time, letting it dissolve before adding the next amount.

Leave the clams to soak in a large bowl of cold water for up to an hour before you use them, moving them around with your hands now and again. The colder the water the better, or the clams might start to open, so add a few ice cubes to cool it down. Change the water a few times to check on the amount of sand that's still emerging from the clams.

Once all the beurre manié is in and the stock has thickened, continue boiling and whisking for a few minutes to cook the flour, or it will taste raw in the chowder. At the end of this time, the liquid will be velvety smooth.

SOLE WITH CAPER
AND LEMON BUTTER

This simple classic is one of the most popular dishes on the menu at the Savoy Grill in London. In the restaurant we use Dover sole, but lemon sole is good too. It's easier to find and much less expensive.

SERVES 2

2 whole lemon sole, weighing about 1lb 2oz (500g) each, gutted, and heads, tails, and skin removed (ask the fishmonger to do this)

1/2 cup all-purpose flour, seasoned with salt and pepper

3 tbsp olive oil

sea salt and freshly milled black pepper

FOR THE CAPER AND LEMON BUTTER

4 tbsp (1/2 stick) unsalted butter

1/3 cup nonpareil capers

juice of 1/2 lemon

2 tbsp roughly chopped fresh curly parsley

Dredge the fish in the seasoned flour.

Put a large, non-stick skillet over high heat, pour in the oil, and heat until hot. Place the fish in the oil and shake the pan to be sure that the fish isn't sticking to it. Leave to cook undisturbed for 4 minutes until golden brown underneath, then turn the fish over and cook undisturbed for 4 minutes longer.

While the fish is cooking, make the caper and lemon butter. Heat a small, non-stick skillet over medium-high heat, add the butter, and wait until it starts to foam. Now stir the butter with a wooden spoon until the foam starts to drop and turn nut brown. Quickly stir in the capers followed by the lemon juice and parsley. Stir vigorously all the time. Remove from the heat and keep hot.

As soon as the fish is done, transfer it to plates and spoon the hot caper and lemon butter over the fish. Serve immediately.

"In a restaurant you can ask for fish to be taken off the bone, but this would be stressful beyond belief to do at home, and the fish would be stone cold by the time you got it to the table. Cooked as it is here, it's very easy just to lift the fish off the bone on your plate with a knife and fork."

KEY TO PERFECTION

Sole is delicate and can quickly overcook and become dry. Coating the fish with flour and pan-frying it whole on the bone is the best way to get moist flesh with a just-cooked flavor. You also need to know the right moment to remove the fish from the pan.

Spread the flour out on a baking sheet and season with salt and pepper. Dip each fish in the flour until thickly and evenly coated on both sides, then pat and shake off the excess.

The side of the fish that was cooked first will be an even golden color when the fish is turned over. This is the flour that has formed a protective coating against the hot oil, preventing the fish from being overcooked.

To check the fish is done, tease the flesh away from the bone with a metal spatula at the thickest point along the central line. Perfectly cooked fish will come away from the bone easily, without scraping or tugging.

CREAMY FISH PIE

Many kinds of fish and shellfish can be used in this potato-topped pie. I like to include shrimp because they add texture to the soft white fish, and they have such a well-defined shellfish flavor. Sometimes I use mussels for a change from shrimp. Another favorite combination is smoked fish, white fish, and shrimp.

SERVES 4

1¼ cups cold Fish Stock (page 45)
2 small sprigs of fresh thyme
1 bay leaf, cut in half
2 celery ribs, strings removed and finely diced
1 small white onion, cut into ¾in (2cm) dice
1 leek (white part only), cut crosswise into ½in (1cm) rounds
10 raw, very large shrimp, preferably tiger prawns, in their shells
1¾ cups whole milk, plus a little extra if needed
1lb 2oz (500g) skinless, thick white fish fillets (cod or haddock), cut into 1¼in (3cm) cubes
leaves of 1 small bunch of fresh flat-leaf parsley, coarsely chopped
2½ cups hot Béchamel Sauce (opposite)
sea salt and freshly milled white pepper

FOR THE TOPPING

1 quantity hot Mashed Potatoes (page 98)
2 extra large egg yolks, preferably organic
1 whole nutmeg, for grating

Pour the stock into a medium saucepan and add 1 sprig of thyme, a piece of bay leaf, and some salt and pepper. Bring to a boil over high heat. Add the celery, onion, and leek, and turn down the heat to medium. Simmer uncovered for 8–10 minutes until tender, then remove from the heat. With a slotted spoon, transfer the vegetables to a colander set over a bowl. Drain the vegetables, then dry well. Pour the drained-off liquid into the stock in the pan and reserve.

Peel the shrimp and halve lengthwise. Devein and rinse the shrimp briefly under cold water. Bring the stock back to a boil and drop in the shrimp. Cover and simmer for 1½ minutes until they all turn pink. Remove the shrimp with a slotted spoon, drain, and dry well. Reserve the stock.

Next cook the fish. Bring the milk to a boil in a clean pan with the remaining thyme and bay leaf and some salt and pepper. Add the fish and bring back to a boil, then take off the heat and leave to stand for 4–5 minutes. Remove the fish with a slotted spoon, drain, and dry well. Strain the reserved stock and milk into a large measuring cup and add more milk if necessary to make 2½ cups. Use for the béchamel sauce.

Gently mix the vegetables, shrimp, and fish together, then divide among four individual ovenproof dishes (or use one large baking dish). Sprinkle with the parsley, then gradually ladle the hot béchamel sauce on top until it reaches the same level as the filling. Don't mix the sauce through or it will break up the fish.

Preheat the oven to 400°F (200°C). Place the ovenproof dishes or baking dish on a baking sheet.

Beat the mashed potatoes with the egg yolks and cool slightly, then transfer to a pastry bag fitted with a ½in (1cm) plain tip. Pipe on top of the fish mixture, and grate nutmeg over the top. Bake for 20–25 minutes (about 35 minutes for a large pie) until the topping is tinged golden brown and the filling is bubbling. Serve hot.

BÉCHAMEL SAUCE

MAKES ABOUT 2 1/2 CUPS
4 tbsp (1/2 stick) unsalted butter
1/4 cup all-purpose flour
2 1/2 cups mixed milk and stock
(from Fish Pie, opposite)
4 tbsp heavy cream
sea salt and freshly milled
white pepper

This recipe uses a combination of milk and fish stock, because this gives a good flavor to the fish pie; a basic béchamel sauce is made with milk only.

Melt the butter in a heavy saucepan over medium-high heat until foaming. Sprinkle in the flour and stir constantly for 3–4 minutes to make a light golden paste or roux. Add the milk and stock to the roux in five stages, beating and whisking until smooth before adding the next stage. When all the liquid has been incorporated, turn the heat down to low and cook for 6–8 minutes longer, whisking regularly. Remove from the heat, stir in the cream, and add seasoning to taste.

KEY TO PERFECTION

The vegetables, shrimp, and fish must be completely dry before they are mixed with the sauce. If they are wet, they will dilute the sauce and make the pie watery.

In turn, as they are cooked, spread the drained vegetables, shrimp, and fish out on a clean, dry cloth (or sheets of paper towel) and pat them thoroughly dry.

STEAMED COD WITH PERFUMED BROTH

I always associate steamed fish with the bland food that people eat when they're not feeling well or are on a diet. This recipe is the exact opposite of that, because it adds flavor to the fish in the most fantastic way. When you smell the aromas of the broth wafting through your kitchen, you'll know exactly what I mean.

SERVES 2
1 large bunch of fresh basil
2 portions of cod fillets, with
   skin on, weighing about
   7oz (200g) each
extra-virgin olive oil, for drizzling
sea salt and freshly milled
   black pepper

FOR THE BROTH
30 coriander seeds
20 white peppercorns
1 star anise
1 tbsp sea salt
2 cups cold Fish Stock (page 45)
2 cups cold Vegetable Nage
   (page 22)
3 stems of lemongrass, roughly
   sliced on the diagonal
pared zest and juice of 2 lemons
20 sprigs of fresh cilantro
10 sprigs of fresh basil
10 sprigs of fresh flat-leaf parsley

First make the broth. Crush the coriander seeds, peppercorns, star anise, and salt together with a heavy knife or in a mortar and pestle. Put them in a pan that is the same diameter as your steamer basket and add the remaining broth ingredients. Bring to a boil over high heat, then cover the pan and boil the broth for 10 minutes. This will get the scent going so the broth will impart flavor to the fish.

Make a bed of basil leaves in the steamer basket. Season and oil the fish well, then nestle the fillets in the basil and put the lid on the basket. Place it on top of the pan of boiling broth, turn the heat down to a brisk simmer, and steam for 8 minutes until the skin will peel easily off the fish.

Skin the hot cod, then sprinkle with sea salt and freshly milled pepper and drizzle with olive oil. Serve immediately.

"Be generous with the amount of salt you sprinkle on the skin. You're not going to eat it, because the skin is coming off, but the flavor will permeate the fish like cooking in a salt crust."

KEY TO PERFECTION

Like many other white fish, cod has a flaky texture and a tendency to fall apart. Gentle steaming is one of the best ways to cook it, and leaving the skin on helps hold it together.

Season the fish and fold in half with the skin on the outside, then sprinkle generously with salt and drizzle with olive oil before placing in the basil-lined steamer. As the fish cooks, the skin will act as a natural protective layer over the delicate flesh.

With your fingers, carefully peel away the skin to reveal the juicy, perfectly cooked white fish underneath. Throw away the skin before serving—steamed skin is flabby, so not good to eat.

SALT AND PEPPER SHRIMP

Tiger prawns and soft-shell crabs are my favorite first courses in an Asian restaurant—it's hard to choose between them. These shrimp in tempura batter are easy to make at home, and they're great to serve as canapés with drinks before dinner.

SERVES 4

16 raw, large shrimp, preferably tiger prawns, in their shells
1/2 cup all-purpose flour
vegetable oil, for deep-frying
sea salt and finely cracked black pepper

FOR THE TEMPURA BATTER

1/3 cup all-purpose flour
1/3 cup cornstarch
1/4 tsp baking soda
2/3 cup ice-cold sparkling water
2 ice cubes
1 extra large egg white, preferably organic, lightly whisked until frothy

TO SERVE

2 tsp Thai sweet chili sauce, or to taste
4 tbsp good-quality mayonnaise
1 hot red chili, deseeded and finely chopped
2 scallions, finely chopped

First make a dip to serve with the shrimp by mixing the chili sauce into the mayonnaise. Keep in a covered bowl in the refrigerator.

Peel the shrimp and cut in half lengthwise. Devein, then rinse briefly under cold water. Don't worry if the shrimp are wet—this will help the flour stick to them.

Spread the flour out on a baking sheet, sprinkle with a little salt and plenty of pepper, and stir well to mix. Toss the shrimp in the seasoned flour until evenly coated, then shake off the excess.

Make the tempura batter by sifting the flour, cornstarch, and baking soda into a bowl. Add the water, ice, and egg white, and whisk gently just to mix. Season with a little salt.

Heat oil in a wok or deep-fat fryer to 325°F (170°C). To test the oil without a thermometer, dip a shrimp in the batter and drop into the hot oil—if the batter crisps up within 2–3 minutes, the oil is hot enough.

Drop about one-third of the shrimp into the batter and stir gently to coat, then take them out with a slotted spoon and lower them one at a time into the hot oil. Deep-fry for 2–3 minutes until the batter becomes crisp and light golden in color. Lift out with a slotted spoon and drain on paper towels; keep hot in a low oven while frying the remaining shrimp in two batches. Be sure to let the oil temperature return to 325°F (170°C) each time.

Serve sprinkled with sea salt, chopped chili, and scallions, with the bowl of chili mayonnaise alongside.

"Don't try to deep-fry all the shrimp at once. This will lower the temperature of the oil and the batter will not crisp up."

KEY TO PERFECTION

Sparkling water and baking soda make tempura batter as light as air. The secret is to work fast and not overmix, or you'll knock out the sparkle.

Add the water and ice cubes to the dry ingredients and immediately start whisking. You need to mix everything together as quickly as possible.

Whisk just until the ingredients come together. Don't try to whisk the lumps out—they will disappear when the batter is cooked.

SHOP FOR FRESH INGREDIENTS ON THE DAY

"Buy only as much as you need, and take time to find the best."

CRAB AND FISH CAKES

When I was young I absolutely hated fish cakes, but when I started eating out in London in my twenties, and had them at The Ivy, my opinion changed. I've perfected this recipe over the years, to create a fish cake that is soft and fluffy and crab-flavored inside, with a crisp, crunchy coating.

SERVES 4

11oz (300g) cod or haddock fillet, skin on
olive oil, for drizzling
11oz (300g) fresh crab meat, picked over for shells and cartilage and patted dry
leaves of 1 small bunch of fresh flat-leaf parsley, finely chopped
½ cup Fish Stock (page 45)
½ cup heavy cream
2 shallots, very finely diced
1 celery rib, strings removed and very finely diced
½ leek (white part only), very finely diced
3 large baking potatoes such as russet or Burbank, about 1lb 2oz (500g) in total, peeled and cut into ¾in (2cm) dice
vegetable oil, for frying
sea salt and freshly milled white pepper

FOR THE COATING

⅔ cup all-purpose flour, seasoned with salt and pepper
2 extra large eggs, preferably organic, beaten
¾ cup plain dried bread crumbs

Preheat the oven to 375°F (190°C). Put the fish skin side down on an oiled baking sheet, season, and drizzle with a little olive oil. Roast for 10 minutes until the fish flakes easily but remains moist. Leave to cool, then take off the skin. Check there are no bones before flaking the fish and mixing with the crab meat and parsley.

Boil the stock in a pan until reduced by half. Add the cream and bring back to a boil, then reduce to a thick coating consistency (about 4 tbsp), stirring often. Cover with plastic wrap and leave to cool.

Heat a little olive oil in another pan and soften the shallots, celery, and leek for 4–5 minutes without coloring. Season, then cool on paper towels. Add the vegetables to the fish.

Put the potatoes in a pan of cold salted water over high heat. Bring to a boil, then turn the heat down, cover, and simmer gently (don't boil) for 15–20 minutes until soft. Drain the potatoes, pour into a large bowl, and crush with a fork. Cool, then gently fold through the fish mixture followed by the cooled reduced sauce, a little at a time. Cover the bowl with plastic wrap and refrigerate for at least an hour.

Form the mixture into eight cakes, then make them neater if you like by shaping them with a 4in (10cm) pastry cutter. Refrigerate for at least 10 minutes to firm up the shape, then coat in the seasoned flour, beaten eggs, and bread crumbs. Refrigerate again for at least 10 minutes to firm up the coating.

Heat ½in (1cm) vegetable oil in a non-stick skillet over high heat until hot. Fry the fish cakes for 4 minutes on each side, basting frequently with the hot oil. Lift out with a slotted metal spatula, drain, and serve, sprinkled with sea salt.

"Be gentle when mixing the fish, potatoes, and sauce together. You want a nice chunky mixture, not a purée."

KEY TO PERFECTION

Fish cakes won't hold together during frying if there's too much moisture in the mixture, so you must get the crab and potatoes really dry before combining them with the vegetables and sauce. Then you need to have a thick coating of bread crumbs to seal everything in.

Crab is always wet, so spread it out on a cloth and pat it thoroughly dry. You can use a kitchen towel or paper towels, whichever you prefer.

When draining the diced potatoes, shake the colander and keep turning the potatoes over with a spoon so they become dry and fluffy.

Coat the cakes in a thick layer of bread crumbs after dusting with flour and dipping in egg. These three layers form a protective coating around the soft fish and potato mixture during cooking, which helps prevent the fish cakes from breaking up.

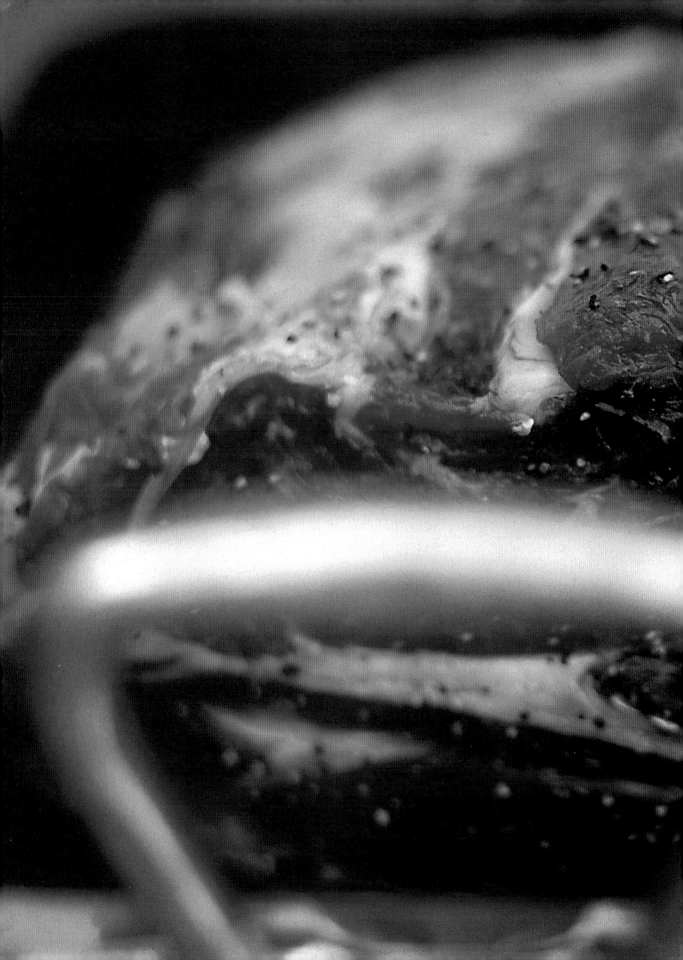

MEAT

ROAST RIB OF BEEF

Sunday is the one day in the week I'm at home and can spend time with my wife and sons. When family and friends come over, I love to cook a rib roast for dinner. I was brought up eating beef that was very well done, because my Dad liked it that way, but now I always cook it rare. When Dad's around, I carve off the first end slices just for him.

SERVES 8

1 beef rib roast with 4 bones, weighing about 12½lb (5.8kg), boned and weighing about 10lb (4.6kg) after boning (ask the butcher for the bones and get him to chop them), or buy a 10lb (4.6kg) boneless roast and 2½lb (1kg) beef ribs for barbecue, chopped into pieces
3 tbsp vegetable oil
sea salt and cracked black pepper

FOR THE GRAVY

1 large yellow onion, roughly chopped
2 carrots, peeled and roughly chopped
2 celery ribs, roughly chopped
2 garlic cloves, lightly crushed
a few sprigs of fresh or dried thyme
7 tbsp all-purpose flour
4 cups hot Beef Stock (page 11)

The beef should be at room temperature when it is put into the oven, so take it out of the refrigerator 1–2 hours before cooking.

Preheat the oven to 400°F (200°C).

Score the fat on top of the beef in a tight diamond pattern, using a very sharp knife. Season the roast well on all sides. Heat the oil in a very large, heavy roasting pan over high heat on top of the stove and sear the roast until evenly browned on all sides.

Remove the meat from the pan. Put the chopped bones in the pan, then sit the roast on top with the fat side up.

Roast the beef for 2 hours, basting well every 15 minutes, until a thermometer registers 130°F (55°C) in the thickest part of the meat.

Transfer the meat to a carving board, cover loosely with foil, and let stand in a warm place for 25–30 minutes.

Make the gravy while the meat is resting. Carefully transfer the contents of the pan to a colander, leaving behind about 1 tsp fat in the pan. Put the pan over high heat on top of the stove. Add the onion, carrots, celery, garlic, and thyme, and color for about 5 minutes, then return the drained bones to the pan and sprinkle with the flour. Turn the bones to make sure they're well coated. Cook for about 5 minutes to color the flour, then pour in about one-third of the hot stock and bubble to reduce. Pour in the remaining stock, stir well, and bring to a boil. Simmer until reduced to the consistency you like. Strain through a colander, then taste and adjust the seasoning.

Slice the beef thickly and arrange the slices overlapping on a warmed platter. Ladle some of the gravy over the beef and serve the rest separately in a gravy boat.

KEY TO PERFECTION

Roast beef should be crisp and well colored on the outside, juicy and deep pink within. To get this perfect result, the secret is to sear it at the beginning of cooking.

ALL IS NOT LOST

If the bones are too darkly colored at the end of cooking the meat, you can't use them to make gravy because they will make it taste bitter. For a quick fix, throw the bones away and use a clean pan to color the vegetables in olive oil, then boost the flavor by pouring in about $\frac{1}{2}$ cup red wine and reduce before adding the stock.

Get the oil in the pan really hot, then put in the roast with its fat side facing down. Leave undisturbed until well colored underneath, then turn the roast on one of its sides and baste with the hot oil. Leave undisturbed again, until the second side is colored.

Repeat the turning, basting, and searing until the whole joint is browned on all four sides and the two ends. The total searing time should be about 20 minutes.

"The chopped bones from the roast make a natural trivet for the meat to cook on, as well as giving flavor to the gravy."

ROAST CHICKEN

I learned this way of cooking a perfect roast chicken at Guy Savoy in Paris. There they used a *poulet de Bresse*, considered to be the king of chickens in France because of its gamey flavor and succulent meat. An organic or free-range bird is the best substitute for *poulet de Bresse*.

SERVES 4

1 chicken, preferably organic or free-range, weighing about 3¼ lb (1.5kg)

2 red onions, quartered lengthwise

2 white onions, quartered lengthwise

4 carrots, peeled and cut into chunks

1 bulb garlic, cut crosswise in half

a few sprigs of fresh or dried thyme

1 organic lemon, cut lengthwise into wedges

½ cup olive oil

30 fresh sage leaves, finely sliced

3 cups hot Chicken Stock (page 16)

2 tbsp cornstarch (optional)

sea salt and freshly milled black pepper

Preheat the oven to 425°F (220°C).

Remove any string and giblets from the chicken, then wipe the cavity clean with paper towels and season inside with a large pinch of salt and a few twists of pepper. Put the onions, carrots, garlic, thyme, and lemon wedges in a roasting pan, season with salt and pepper, and stir in half the olive oil.

Sit the chicken breast-side up on top of the vegetables. Drizzle with the rest of the olive oil and sprinkle with salt and pepper. Roast for 1 hour 20 minutes, turning the bird regularly and basting with the cooking juices.

To check if the chicken is done, insert a skewer or the tip of a sharp, narrow-bladed knife deep into the thick end of a thigh. The bird is cooked if the juices run clear; if there are any traces of blood you will need to carry on cooking until they are gone.

When the chicken is cooked, transfer it to a carving board and cover loosely with foil. Let stand in a warm place for 10–15 minutes.

Remove the garlic, thyme, and lemon from the vegetables, then transfer the vegetables to a bowl with a slotted spoon and stir the sage leaves through them. Keep warm.

Strain the cooking liquid from the roasting pan into a saucepan. Pour in the stock and bring to a boil, then simmer until reduced to about 2½ cups. If you would like a thicker sauce, mix the cornstarch to a paste with 2 tbsp cold water, pour it into the pan, and boil for a few minutes, whisking constantly until thickened. Taste and adjust the seasoning, then pour the sauce into a gravy boat.

Carve the chicken and serve with the vegetables and sauce.

"Use the vegetables to prop the chicken up when it's roasting on its side. This will keep it from tumbling over."

KEY TO PERFECTION

For juicy, melt-in-the-mouth chicken, you need to turn the bird over several times and baste it well during roasting. This helps the heat penetrate evenly and makes the meat moist.

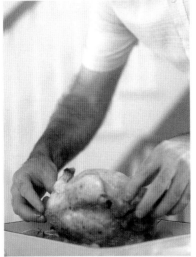

After the chicken has been roasting for half an hour, and the skin on the breast is nicely colored and crisp, turn the bird onto one of its sides and baste well. Roast for 10 minutes, then turn the bird onto its other side. Baste and return to the oven to roast for another 10 minutes.

Now turn the chicken over onto its breast, so the back is facing up, and baste well. Return to the oven to roast for another 10 minutes. Finally, sit the bird breast-side up and roast for the remainder of the time.

PAN-GRILLED LAMB CHOPS

A heavy, ridged grill pan is a relatively new addition to the home kitchen. I couldn't manage without mine. It's the perfect way to cook chops and steaks because the meat sits on the ridges of the pan and the fat runs down into the grooves in between.

SERVES 2
6–8 loin lamb chops
olive oil, for brushing
6–8 sprigs of fresh rosemary
sea salt and freshly milled
**   black pepper**

FOR THE MINT SAUCE
1 tbsp red currant jelly
3 tbsp malt vinegar
1/4 cup finely chopped fresh
**   mint leaves**

TO SERVE
Spinach with Garlic and Cream
**   (page 108)**

First make the mint sauce. Melt the jelly over low heat in a small pan. Remove from the heat and stir in the vinegar. Leave to cool before adding the mint. Use the sauce as soon as possible (within an hour of making it) or the mint will discolor.

Brush the meat lightly with olive oil. Season the fat and meat with salt and pepper.

Heat a dry grill pan over high heat until very hot. Stand the chops on their fatty edges in the pan and cook for 4–5 minutes until the fat renders and the edges becomes crisp.

Lay the chops flat on one of their sides and strew the rosemary sprigs all over the meat. Cook for another 4–5 minutes, basting frequently with the fat in the pan.

Turn the chops over and cook the other sides for the same length of time, basting as before.

Arrange the chops on a bed of spinach on each plate and serve immediately, with the mint sauce in a small bowl.

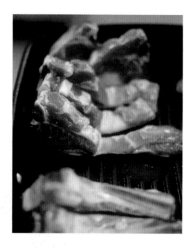

KEY TO PERFECTION

Rendering the fat in a grill pan at the beginning of cooking will give the chops a crisp edge, then you can use the melted fat for basting the meat as it continues to cook. This will make the meat naturally moist and juicy, without the need for a lot of extra oil or fat.

Using tongs, stand the chops on their fat edges in the grill pan, leaning them against the sides and each other for support. As the fat melts, it will run down between the ridges of the pan.

ROAST BELLY OF PORK
WITH APPLES AND ONIONS

For the moistest roast pork around, head to a Chinese or Italian butcher and ask for pork belly. This cut is becoming a favorite of restaurant chefs, and deserves to be cooked at home more often, too. It is a fatty cut, but much of the fat will render out during roasting.

SERVES 6

1 piece of boneless pork belly, weighing about 4¹/₂lb (2kg), skin finely scored on the diagonal across its width
1 heaped tbsp fine table salt
2 yellow onions, cut lengthwise into wedges
3 Granny Smith apples, cut lengthwise into wedges and cores removed
6–8 sprigs of fresh thyme
olive oil, for drizzling
coarse sea salt (such as Maldon), or kosher salt, and freshly milled white pepper

Trim off and discard any excess fat from the meaty side of the belly. Wipe the skin thoroughly dry, then rub half the fine salt into the skin and in between the score lines. Set aside for about 30 minutes.

Preheat the oven to 350°F (180°C).

Put the onion and apple wedges in a heavy roasting pan along with the thyme, a drizzle of oil, and a good sprinkling of salt and pepper. Put the pork on top of the onions and apples and wipe the skin dry again. Sprinkle the remaining fine salt over the skin and drizzle with oil. Massage these in well, then sprinkle with coarse sea salt.

Place the roasting pan in the hottest part of the oven and roast for 1¹/₂ hours. Increase the temperature to 400°F (200°C) and roast for a further 45 minutes to 1 hour until the skin is crisp. Remove the pork from the oven and let stand in a warm place for about 15 minutes.

Remove the skin and cut into thin strips, then carve the meat crosswise into neat slices. Serve the pork and skin on warmed plates, with some of the roasted onion and apple.

"Crisp skin comes from two sorts of salt. Fine salt brings out the moisture, then coarse sea salt creates a nice crust."

KEY TO PERFECTION

Pork has less fat and is wetter than it used to be, which makes it more difficult to get crisp skin. Scoring the skin finely will help overcome this, as will drying and salting the skin before roasting.

Pat the skin thoroughly dry with a clean cloth or a wad of paper towels. When the scored skin is dry, it will blister and crisp in the heat of the oven.

Sprinkle fine salt over the skin, then rub it into both the skin and the incisions. The salt will draw water out of the skin so that after it's been standing for half an hour you'll see beads of moisture collecting on the skin's surface.

ALL IS NOT LOST

If your pork skin isn't quite crisp enough at the end of roasting, remove it from the pork in one piece, turn it upside down on a board, and scrape off the fat beneath using a spoon. Put it roasted side up on a baking sheet lined with parchment paper and place in the hottest part of the oven to crisp for about 10 minutes.

BEEF HOTPOT

In England, a hotpot is a rich, savory stew covered with a lid of sliced potatoes. The most famous is Lancashire hotpot, made with tender lamb and its kidneys. My version here uses beef, and the result is satisfying, substantial, and delicious.

SERVES 6

3¼ lb (1.5kg) chuck steak, diced
about 1 cup all-purpose flour,
    seasoned with salt and
    pepper, for coating
olive oil, for frying
1 yellow onion, finely sliced
2 carrots, peeled and finely sliced
1 garlic clove, finely sliced
4 cups hot Beef Stock (page 11)
2 tbsp fresh thyme leaves
3–4 medium to large Yukon Gold
    potatoes, about 1½ lb (700g)
    total weight
4 tbsp (½ stick) unsalted butter,
    melted
sea salt and freshly milled
    black pepper

Preheat the oven to 350°F (180°C).

Coat the meat with seasoned flour. Put a large, deep, non-stick skillet over high heat. Pour in enough oil just to cover the bottom of the pan and heat until the oil is hot. Fry the meat in three batches until well colored on all sides, adding more oil to the pan if and when needed. Remove the last batch of meat from the pan, then fry the onion, carrots, and garlic until colored.

Put the meat back in the pan with the vegetables, pour in the stock, and stir well. Bring to a boil. Add salt and pepper and half the thyme, and stir well again. Remove from the heat and divide the beef and vegetables equally among six individual ovenproof dishes (each about 3-cup capacity).

Peel the potatoes and slice into ⅛in (3mm) thick disks. Arrange the disks on top of the beef and vegetables, overlapping them slightly. Brush the potatoes with the melted butter, and sprinkle with salt and pepper and the remaining thyme leaves.

Cover the dishes with lids or foil and bake for 1 hour, then uncover and bake for 45 minutes longer until the meat feels tender when pierced with the tip of a small, sharp knife. Serve hot.

KEY TO PERFECTION

For a richly flavored hotpot with a good color and gravy with substance, the meat needs to be coated in flour and fried until browned at the beginning. Always work in small batches when you're frying meat so you don't overfill the pan—this would make the temperature drop and the meat would stew, not fry.

Put about one-third of the meat in a bowl and sprinkle with one-third of the seasoned flour. Toss with your hands until the meat is evenly coated, then remove and shake off the excess flour. Repeat until all the meat has been coated in this way.

Fry each batch of beef in a single layer in the hot oil until colored underneath. Resist the urge to turn or prod the meat until it's brown—the less you interfere with it, the sooner it will color. Once the meat is crisp and browned underneath, turn and repeat on the other sides until the cubes are browned all over. Don't rush this stage or the flour will taste raw in the stew—each batch should take 7–10 minutes.

BRAISED PORK CHOPS

Most pork chops are lean these days, which means they can be tough and chewy—but not if they're cooked according to this recipe that I learned from my mother. The secrets for juicy, tender chops are to use lots of onions and braise long and slow.

SERVES 4

4 pork loin chops, weighing
   7–8oz (200–225g) each
2 large yellow onions, peeled
6–8 sprigs of fresh thyme
15 fresh sage leaves
2 tsp dried sage
4 tbsp (½ stick) cold unsalted
   butter, diced
sea salt and freshly milled
   black pepper

Preheat the oven to 350°F (180°C).

Place the chops in a single layer in a heavy baking dish.
Season well. Cut the onions in half lengthwise, then turn them on their cut sides and cut crosswise into thin slices. Cover the chops with the onions, separating the slices as you scatter them. Top with the thyme sprigs, fresh and dried sage, and butter. Season well.

Cover the dish with a tight-fitting lid or seal with foil. Bake for about 1½ hours, basting occasionally, until the pork feels tender when pierced with the tip of a sharp knife.

Serve the chops with the onions piled on top, and the buttery juices spooned over and around.

KEY TO PERFECTION

During the long, slow cooking, the onions give off sweet, natural juices that join forces with the fat from the chops and the butter. This makes a natural sauce, and the meat becomes juicy, tender, and full of flavor.

You need piles of thinly sliced onions and lots of butter to start with. The chops should be completely buried in the onions, so their juices will seep into the chops with the melted butter during cooking.

As the onions soften and the chops gently cook beneath them, juices collect in the bottom of the dish. Two or three times during cooking, remove the lid or foil and tilt the dish so the juices run into one corner. Scoop up the juices with a spoon and drizzle them over the onions and chops.

"Don't worry about the chops overcooking—you need to allow time for the onion juices to be absorbed by the meat. This is the very best way to get tender pork chops."

SAUSAGES WITH ONION GRAVY

Sausages smothered in a thick gravy loaded with onions is just the kind of thing that my Mom would serve for dinner, and I still love it. This recipe is my variation on hers—with a marinade and a touch of red wine. You can use herb or Italian-seasoned pork sausages.

SERVES 4
8 large, fresh pork sausages
2 tbsp olive oil
2 red onions, sliced ¼in
   (5mm) thick
3 yellow onions, sliced ¼in
   (5mm) thick
2 garlic cloves, finely chopped
a few sprigs of fresh or
   dried thyme
1 cup red wine or stout
2 bay leaves
1 sprig of fresh or dried rosemary
2 cups hot Beef Stock (page 11)
a handful of fresh curly
   parsley, chopped
sea salt and freshly milled
   white pepper

FOR THE MARINADE
2 tbsp olive oil
a few sprigs of fresh
   or dried thyme
2 garlic cloves, chopped

Mix the sausages and marinade ingredients in a self-sealing plastic bag and shake well. Refrigerate for 2 hours, or overnight.

Put a large wok or deep, non-stick skillet over low to medium heat. When the pan is hot, pour in the contents of the bag and fry for 10–15 minutes until the sausages are golden brown on all sides. Remove the sausages from the pan with a slotted spoon.

Pour the oil into the pan and heat until very hot. Add the onions, garlic, and thyme, stir well, and season with a large pinch of salt and a few twists of pepper. Cook over medium to high heat for about 10 minutes, stirring occasionally, until the onions are caramelized. Meanwhile, boil the wine in a small, heavy saucepan until it has reduced by about one-third.

Pour the wine over the onions and stir in the bay leaves and rosemary. Continue cooking for another 10 minutes, stirring frequently, until the onions are gooey and red.

Add the stock to the onions and mix well, then bring to a boil. Return the sausages to the pan. Turn the heat down to a gentle simmer, cover, and cook for 35 minutes, stirring occasionally.

Throw in the parsley and check the seasoning before serving.

"Lincolnshire sausages are my favorite, so I always like to use them for this dish. They are quite spicy, which is why I season the dish with white pepper rather than black. White pepper is milder."

KEY TO PERFECTION

Using lots of onions gives body to the gravy, while reducing them down brings out their sweetness. This will make the sausages moist and juicy.

For the best-ever gravy, you must start off with a full pan of onions. Don't think you can get away with any less. Using both red and white onions gives extra flavor as well as color.

Cook the onions with the red wine, stirring occasionally, until they reduce down to a gooey mass. The flavor will become more concentrated as the onions shrink, and the color will turn a deep burgundy red.

STEAK AU POIVRE

When I started out as a chef, I worked with my brother Brian in our hometown, and steak au poivre was a mainstay on the menu. We always flambéed it tableside, but at home you can skip the flaming bit and still enjoy this French bistro classic. Black peppercorns are the traditional coating, but they're a little too coarse and hot for me, so I've mellowed them by mixing in green and white peppercorns.

SERVES 4

4 tournedos (thick filet mignon steaks cut from the center of the tenderloin and tied with string), weighing about 7oz (200g) each
1 tbsp dried green peppercorns
1 tsp black peppercorns
1/2 tsp white peppercorns
pinch of sea salt
4 tsp Dijon mustard
3 tbsp olive oil
5 tbsp cold unsalted butter, diced
Pommes Mousseline (page 100), to serve

Take the steaks out of the refrigerator about half an hour before you want to cook them.

Preheat the oven to 400°F (200°C).

Coarsely crush the peppercorns and salt in a mortar and pestle. Coat the steaks with the mustard, then with the peppercorns.

Put a large ovenproof skillet over high heat. When hot, pour in the oil and heat until it is hot, then fry the steaks until they are seared all over. Add the diced butter and let it melt into the hot oil—it will calm everything down and turn the fat and juices a nut-brown color (called *beurre noisette* in French).

Transfer the pan of steaks to the oven. Roast for 4 minutes for rare meat, 7 minutes for medium. Baste the steaks with the juices in the pan halfway through cooking.

Remove the steaks from the oven and let them stand in a warm place for about 4 minutes.

Snip the string off the steaks, then cut each steak into four even slices. Arrange on plates, drizzle with the pan juices, and serve the potatoes alongside.

"If you prefer your steaks less peppery, just put peppercorns on the top of each steak, or on the top and bottom. You could also use Sichuan peppercorns instead of the white or green. They are perfumed and spicy rather than hot, and will make a slightly milder-tasting crust."

KEY TO PERFECTION

To get peppered steaks cooked exactly how you like them, the combination of pan-frying and roasting gives the best results. If you pan-fry the steaks for the whole cooking time, the peppercorns will scorch and turn bitter.

Brush mustard evenly all over the steaks. This will give the peppercorns a sticky surface to cling to, as well as adding extra flavor to the meat.

Roll the steaks in the crushed peppercorns on a flat surface, and pat them firmly with your hands to make sure they stick evenly. They should cover the sides of each steak, and the top and bottom.

For accurate cooking, sear the steaks in the hot oil for exactly 6 minutes (1 minute on each side and 1 minute each for the top and bottom). The roasting time in the oven then varies, according to how well you like your steak cooked—rare or medium.

SICHUAN CHICKEN

If I want something simple to cook for my sons, it's almost always Chinese or chicken. This is one of my favorite stir-fries because I can make it from things we've got in the refrigerator or pantry.

SERVES 4

4 skinless, boneless chicken
   breast halves, cut diagonally
   into 1/4in (5mm) thick strips
2in (5cm) piece of fresh ginger,
   peeled and minced
2 garlic cloves, minced
4 tbsp vegetable oil
1 carrot, peeled and pared into
   ribbons with a vegetable peeler
1 tsp Asian dark sesame oil
2 heads of baby bok choy, roots
   sliced off and leaves separated
5 scallions, cut diagonally
   into strips
1 tsp Sichuan peppercorns,
   lightly crushed
sea salt
fresh cilantro leaves, to finish

FOR THE MARINADE

1/2 cup dark soy sauce
1/2 cup mirin (sweet rice wine)
3–4 tbsp sake (rice wine)
2 tbsp light brown sugar

Mix all the marinade ingredients together in a bowl, add the chicken strips, and stir to coat. Cover and leave for half an hour, or in the refrigerator for up to 24 hours.

When you're ready to cook, drain the chicken in a colander set over a bowl; reserve the marinade. Mix the ginger and garlic into the chicken. Put a wok or large, deep skillet over high heat. When hot, pour in the oil and heat until you can see a light haze rising.

Toss in the chicken and leave undisturbed for 2 minutes until colored underneath, then shake the pan and turn the chicken over. Leave the chicken to sit undisturbed for another 2 minutes until it is colored on the other side. Remove the chicken with a slotted spoon and set aside.

Add the carrot ribbons to the pan followed by the sesame oil and a pinch of salt. Toss for a minute, then tip in the chicken and its juices, the bok choy, scallions, and crushed peppercorns. Finish by splashing in some of the marinade and simmering for 3–4 minutes.

Before serving, taste and add more salt or soy sauce if you like, and toss in the cilantro leaves.

KEY TO PERFECTION

Chicken breast is very lean, which means it can be bland and dry. Steeping it in a marinade will give it flavor and succulence. The longer you leave it the better, but even as little as half an hour can make a difference.

When you add the chicken to the bowl of marinade, turn the strips so they are evenly coated in the liquid. Then, to make sure the strips get maximum penetration from the liquid and flavorings, stir them as often as you remember during the marinating time.

"You can change the vegetables in this recipe according to what you have in the salad drawer of your refrigerator. Spinach, bell peppers, broccoli, beans, snow peas, and celery are all good."

CORNED BEEF HASH CAKES

We often make these hash cakes at home, and have them with broiled sausages, bacon, mushrooms, and tomatoes—it makes a great weekend brunch that we all enjoy.

MAKES 8

2¹/₄lb (1kg) Yukon Gold potatoes
fine table salt
4 tbsp (¹/₂ stick) unsalted butter, diced
1 yellow onion, finely chopped
2 garlic cloves, finely chopped
1 large can (about 14oz/400g) corned beef, broken up with a fork
2 tbsp store-bought brown or steak sauce
1 large egg, preferably organic, beaten
about 1 cup unseasoned dried bread crumbs
about ¹/₃ cup all-purpose flour, for coating
olive oil, for frying
sea salt and freshly milled black pepper
duck eggs or large organic hen eggs, to serve

Peel the potatoes and grate on the coarse holes of a box grater. Sprinkle lightly with fine salt, then let stand for 5–10 minutes. Meanwhile, heat the butter in a skillet over high heat until foaming. Add the onion and garlic, season with salt, and cook for 4–5 minutes until soft and golden brown. Remove the pan from the heat.

Now squeeze the moisture out of the potatoes and drop them into a bowl. With your hands, mix in the corned beef, softened onion and garlic, brown sauce, and egg. Add enough bread crumbs to bind the mixture together. Season well.

Divide the corned beef mix into eight equal portions. Shape into cakes and coat in flour. For a neat edge, press each cake into a 4in (10cm) pastry ring. Chill for at least 4 hours, or overnight.

Preheat the oven to 400°F (200°C).

Cover the bottom of a large, non-stick skillet with olive oil and place over high heat. When hot, place the cakes in the pan and fry for about 4 minutes on each side until crisp and golden brown. Transfer the cakes to a baking sheet and bake for 10–15 minutes, turning over halfway. Meanwhile, use the oil in the frying pan to fry as many duck or hen eggs as you like.

Serve the hash cakes hot, topped with the eggs.

"For Sunday brunch, I get the hash mix ready the day before and chill it as a log shape wrapped tightly in plastic wrap. It's then really easy to slice into neat rounds just before frying."

KEY TO PERFECTION

For hash to be crisp and crunchy on the outside, you need to get the potatoes thoroughly dry before shaping and frying the cakes. If the potatoes are wet, water will run out of them into the pan and make the hash soggy.

Put a sieve over a bowl and line with a cloth. Pick up handfuls of grated potato and squeeze hard to extract as much moisture as possible, then drop the potato into the cloth-lined sieve. Sprinkle with salt and mix well.

After 5–10 minutes, the salt will have drawn moisture out of the potatoes and they will look wet again. Pick them up in the cloth and twist the cloth tightly into a ball shape. Squeeze hard to wring out as much water as possible.

Open the cloth to check if the potatoes are dry. If they're not, put them into a clean, dry cloth and wring again.

ALL IS NOT LOST

If the cakes don't hold their shape when you're frying them, press them all into one big cake. Fry until golden brown underneath, then broil until brown on top. Crack 4 eggs into the center and bake for 10 minutes until the eggs are set. Serve sprinkled with chopped fresh thyme, sea salt, and olive oil.

BRAISED LAMB SHANKS

After long, slow cooking, the meat on lamb shanks is so tender it literally falls off the bone. For a neat presentation, ask the butcher to French trim the meat at the bony end to expose the bone, or do it yourself by scraping off the meat and fat with a sharp knife.

SERVES 6

5 tbsp olive oil

6 lamb shanks, each weighing about 1lb (450g)

2 yellow onions, cut into chunks

2 large carrots, peeled and cut into chunks

1 leek (green part only), cut into chunks

4 celery ribs, strings removed and cut into chunks

4 garlic cloves, peeled and left whole

4 fresh or dried sprigs of rosemary

6–8 sprigs of fresh thyme

2 tbsp tomato paste

1¹⁄₂ cups dry white wine

2 quarts (2 liters) hot Chicken Stock (page 16)

sea salt and freshly milled black pepper

finely chopped fresh rosemary, to finish

Preheat the oven to 350°F (180°C).

Heat the oil in a very large, heavy skillet (cast iron is good, but non-stick will do). Season the lamb well and sear over high heat until golden brown underneath before turning and searing on another side. Continue turning and frying until the shanks are nicely colored all over. Don't rush this stage—it is essential for color and flavor in the finished dish. The total searing time should be about 20 minutes. Transfer the shanks to a very large, deep casserole.

In the same oil the meat was seared in, fry the onions, carrots, leeks, celery, and garlic with the sprigs of rosemary and thyme over medium heat for about 5 minutes until lightly colored. Add 1 tsp salt and the tomato paste, stir well, and cook for 3 minutes longer. Pour in the wine and reduce by half, then pour in the stock and bring to a boil.

Ladle the liquid and vegetables over the lamb in the casserole. Cover with a *cartouche* of parchment paper, then braise in the oven for 2–2¹⁄₄ hours. The lamb is done when you can see the meat starting to come away from the bones.

Remove the sprigs of herbs, and check and correct the seasoning of the sauce. Serve in warmed bowls, sprinkled with chopped fresh rosemary.

KEY TO PERFECTION

For lamb that is so moist and tender you can eat it with a spoon, it should be slowly braised in the oven in a covered pan. The secret of success lies in the way it is covered—for this dish, a parchment paper lid called a *cartouche* is most effective.

Press the *cartouche* over the surface of the liquid so that it rests directly on it and becomes wet. The paper prevents the meat from drying out, at the same time as letting some steam escape. This allows the liquid to reduce and create a sauce.

Make the *cartouche* by folding a large rectangle of parchment paper in half lengthwise, then in half crosswise. With the closed corner as the point, fold the paper diagonally in half, then in half again to make a fan shape. Hold the point over the center of the casserole, cut the paper 2in (5cm) larger than the circumference of the pot, and unfold the paper.

VEGETABLES

SPICED EGGPLANT

This dish is similar to *baba ghanoush*, the Middle Eastern dip that is usually chilled and served with toasted pita. It also makes a great hors d'oeuvre spooned onto toasted baguette slices. I thought it might be good as a hot side dish, too, and found that it works amazingly well. It's lovely with lamb or fish, especially red mullet or snapper.

SERVES 4

3 large eggplants
2 large garlic cloves, thinly sliced
2 bay leaves, cut in half
a few sprigs of fresh thyme, snipped into short lengths
2 tbsp tomato paste
1 tbsp mild curry powder
5 tsp ground cumin
4 tbsp olive oil
a handful of fresh cilantro leaves, chopped
sea salt and freshly milled black pepper

Preheat the oven to 400°F (200°C).

Cut the eggplants in half lengthwise with a sharp knife, then make deep incisions in a small diamond pattern in the flesh of each half without cutting through the skin.

Push the garlic slices, bay leaves, and thyme sprigs into the incisions (the handle of a teaspoon is good for this), then spread the tomato paste over the top and sprinkle with the spices. Season with salt and pepper, and drizzle with a little of the oil.

Sandwich the halves back together, then wrap each eggplant tightly in foil, making sure the whole vegetable is covered. Place in a roasting pan and bake for about 1 hour until soft.

Unwrap the eggplants while they're still hot and separate the halves. Using a spoon, scoop and scrape out the flesh into a sieve suspended over a bowl. Pick out and discard the bay leaves and herb stalks. Leave the eggplant flesh to drain for about half an hour, then turn it out onto a cutting board and chop roughly.

Place a large, heavy skillet over high heat. When hot, pour in the remaining oil and heat it until you can see a haze rising. Add the eggplant flesh and cook for about 5 minutes until the mixture becomes darker in color and looks quite dry. Stir in the cilantro, and check and correct the seasoning if necessary. Serve immediately.

"To serve as a dip, once the eggplants have cooled, fold in a couple of spoonfuls of plain yogurt and some chopped fresh mint, then chill well."

KEY TO PERFECTION

The beauty of this dish is the combination of fantastic flavors and silky soft texture.
To get both right, there are two important stages.

Bake the eggplants until they feel
really soft when you squeeze them.
Encasing in foil and cooking for a long
time are essential to allow the flavors
of the herbs, spices, and garlic to
penetrate the deeply scored flesh.

Eggplants give off a lot of liquid, which
will dilute the dish and make it sloppy if
you don't get rid of it. While the baked
flesh is draining, press with a spoon
from time to time, to extract as much
liquid as possible.

UPSIDE-DOWN SHALLOT TARTLETS

If topped with melted goat cheese and served with a salad, these tarts could be a vegetarian main course, or do well as a first course. The contrast between the melt-in-the-mouth, sugary shallots and the crisp, buttery pastry makes them totally irresistible.

SERVES 4

1lb (450g) package all-butter puff pastry, thawed

about 16 even-sized, small shallots

²/₃ cup granulated sugar

5 tbsp (¹/₂ stick plus 1 tbsp) cold unsalted butter, diced

sea salt and freshly milled black pepper

You need four 5in (12.5cm) non-stick individual blini pans, which can be found at specialty kitchenware shops and online. Place them on a baking sheet and set aside.

On a lightly floured surface, bat the block of pastry with a rolling pin a few times to make it thinner and easier to roll evenly, then cut into quarters and roll out each piece until ¹/₈in (3mm) thick. Cut out four disks using a pastry cutter or saucer that is 1in (2.5cm) bigger than the blini pans. Stack the disks on top of each other with waxed paper in between and refrigerate for at least 30 minutes.

Meanwhile, halve the shallots crosswise, then trim them to size. Set aside. Heat the oven to 375°F (190°C). Half fill a roasting pan with cold water and keep by the stove.

Mix the sugar and 3 tbsp cold water in a small, heavy saucepan over medium heat. When the sugar has dissolved, increase the heat to high and cook for 5–10 minutes to an amber-colored caramel. Don't stir or the sugar will crystallize and go grainy, but occasionally brush down the sides of the pan with a pastry brush dipped in cold water — this will help prevent crystallization.

Whisk the cold butter into the caramel a little at a time (it will foam up and thicken the caramel), then take the pan off the heat and add a few twists of pepper. Pour an equal quantity of caramel into each blini pan — it will harden immediately.

Sprinkle a little salt over the caramel, then pack the shallots in the pans with their widest cut sides facing down. The exact number of shallots you need depends on their size and how tightly you pack them in, but you should get about eight halves in each pan.

Prick each pastry disk all over with a fork. Lay a disk over each pan and tuck well in between the shallots and the edge of the pan. Bake for 20–25 minutes until the pastry is an even golden brown.

Leave the tarts to settle for a few minutes, then invert a small plate over each pan and turn out the tart onto the plate. Serve hot.

KEY TO PERFECTION

The shallots must all be trimmed to the same size and thickness. If they're not, they will make the pastry uneven and some will be cooked before others.

Cut the roots and tops off the shallots, then cut each shallot crosswise in half and peel off the skin. Line them up on a board so you can see which ones are taller, then trim them so they are all the same height.

ALL IS NOT LOST

If the caramel starts to color too fast and you think it may scorch, quickly dip the base of the pan in the roasting pan of cold water, and hold it there until the cooking has stopped.

"With puff pastry, even rolling equals even rising, and batting it flat before rolling it out is vital for this. Each time you bat the dough, move it around a quarter turn."

MASHED POTATOES

My version of mashed potatoes is softer and richer than most, with a good amount of butter mixed in. It's great as a pie topping, too, and when it's enriched with egg yolks, it can be piped. You can see it like this on my Fish Pie (pages 50–53).

SERVES 4

2¼lb (1kg) baking potatoes, such as russet or Burbank
large pinch of fine table salt
8 tbsp (1 stick) cold unsalted butter, diced
½–¾ cup hot whole milk
¼ tsp freshly grated nutmeg (optional)
sea salt and freshly milled white pepper

Peel the potatoes and cut into 1½in (4cm) pieces. Put the pieces in a saucepan of cold water, add the fine salt, and bring to a boil over high heat. Lower the heat to medium, cover, and simmer gently (don't boil) for about 20 minutes until soft. Drain well.

Return the potatoes to the pan and dry them out, then remove from the heat and mash until smooth. With a wooden spoon, work the butter into the mash a few pieces at a time, then beat in enough hot milk to give a soft, dropping consistency.

Taste and correct the seasoning if necessary, and add the nutmeg if you like. Serve hot.

KEY TO PERFECTION

For smooth, fluffy mashed potatoes, you must get the potatoes dry after boiling, and mash hard before adding butter and milk.

 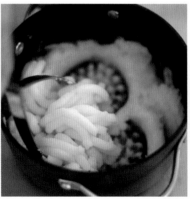 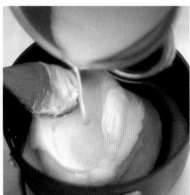

After draining the potatoes, put them back into the pan and let them steam over low heat for a few minutes. Shake the pan and toss the potatoes occasionally so they all become dry.

Work hard with the potato masher—it's important to get the potatoes really smooth at this stage, because mashing becomes more difficult once the butter and milk have been added.

Hot milk is essential—it helps smooth out any imperfections in the mash. Pour it in a little at a time and beat hard until it's absorbed before adding more.

POMMES MOUSSELINE

Here's a very special potato dish that is so velvety and rich it's almost like a mousse—hence its name. It's sheer indulgence, and I love it. I'm sure you will, too.

SERVES 6

2¼lb (1kg) Ratte, fingerling, or Yukon Gold potatoes, washed but not peeled
large pinch of fine table salt
1¼ cups whole milk
1¼ cups heavy cream
7 tbsp (½ stick plus 3 tbsp) cold unsalted butter, diced
sea salt and freshly milled black pepper

Put the potatoes in a saucepan and cover with cold water. Add the fine salt, cover, and bring to a boil, then turn the heat down to medium. Simmer gently (don't boil) for about 30 minutes until the potatoes feel soft when gently squeezed. Remove the pan from the heat.

One at a time, take the potatoes out of the water and peel off the skin with a small, sharp knife. As soon as they're all peeled, push them through a food mill.

Transfer the puréed potatoes to a clean saucepan. Bring the milk and cream to boiling point in another pan, then remove from the heat. Using a rubber spatula, beat one-third of the creamy milk into the potatoes over medium heat, followed by one-third of the butter.

Carry on beating in the milk and butter in two more batches. The potatoes will become shiny and silky smooth. Make sure each batch of milk and butter is fully incorporated before adding the next, and switch to a balloon whisk when the purée gets to the liquid stage. To allow for different varieties of potatoes, you may need to adjust the amounts of milk and butter.

To serve, taste and correct the seasoning if necessary, then pour the potatoes into a warmed bowl.

"We wear thick rubber gloves to protect our hands when peeling cooked potatoes, because the hotter they are, the easier they are to purée. If you let potatoes go cold, they can turn gluey."

KEY TO PERFECTION

For an ultra-smooth purée, you need hot potatoes, hot creamy milk, and a food mill. You can use a large sieve instead of a mill, but it's much harder work, and you need to be careful not to scrape or drag the potatoes across the sieve or they could end up like glue.

Set the mill over a bowl, put in a small quantity of hot potatoes, and turn the handle to press and work them through the perforated base. Repeat until all the potatoes are puréed.

The purée should be as smooth as silk after adding all the hot creamy milk and butter, and runny enough to pour from the pan straight into a bowl.

DRESS THE PART

"Put your apron on and clear your working area, then start assembling all the ingredients and equipment."

ROASTED POTATOES

My Dad used to be a fruit and potato merchant, and potatoes were his passion. His favorites were baking potatoes, because they end up with a dry, fluffy interior. That's just what you want for roasted potatoes, the essential side dish with roast meat and chicken.

SERVES 4
8 large baking potatoes,
   such as russet or Burbank,
   peeled and quartered
fine table salt
1/2 cup vegetable oil
sea salt, to serve

Put the potatoes in a saucepan, cover with cold water, and add 1 1/2 tsp fine salt. Cover and bring to a boil over high heat, then turn the heat down to medium. Simmer gently (don't boil) for 15 minutes until the potatoes are almost cooked. The tip of a small, sharp knife should go in easily without breaking the potato up.

Preheat the oven to 425°F (220°C).

Drain the potatoes in a colander and shake well, then leave to dry out for a few minutes. Meanwhile, heat the oil in a heavy roasting pan in the oven until very hot.

Remove the roasting pan from the oven. One by one, carefully place the potatoes in the oil (don't pour them from the colander into the pan or you'll get splashed with hot oil). Season the potatoes with a large pinch of fine salt and turn them in the oil until they're coated, then return the pan to the oven.

Roast the potatoes for 30–40 minutes until crisp and golden. Turn them every 10 minutes, and sprinkle with sea salt about halfway through when they're starting to color.

Take the potatoes out of the oil with a slotted spoon and drain on paper towels. Serve hot, sprinkled with more sea salt.

KEY TO PERFECTION

Golden and crisp on the outside, soft and fluffy inside—these are the perfect roasted potatoes. To achieve this result, there are two crucial stages.

Once the potatoes are dry, scratch them all over with a fork. By making the flesh rough on the outside, the hot oil will be able to penetrate into the surface quickly, which will make the potatoes crisp.

After boiling and draining, the potatoes must be allowed to dry out. Shake them in the colander to get rid of excess water and lightly break up the outsides, then leave for a few minutes for the steam to escape.

ALL IS NOT LOST

If the potatoes aren't getting crisp enough toward the end of cooking, put the pan over high heat on top of the stove, and toss and turn the potatoes until they crisp up.

SAUTÉED POTATOES

This is the classic French way of sautéing potatoes—with lots of butter. In restaurants they are traditionally served with grilled steak, but they are equally at home with sausages, bacon, and beans.

SERVES 4

16 small red-skinned potatoes, washed but not peeled
1 sprig of fresh or dried thyme
1 garlic clove, lightly crushed
fine table salt
2 tbsp olive oil
7 tbsp (½ stick plus 3 tbsp) cold unsalted butter, diced
sea salt

Put the potatoes in a saucepan, cover with cold water, and add the thyme, garlic, and a large pinch of fine salt. Cover the pan and bring to a boil over high heat, then turn the heat down to medium and simmer gently (don't boil) for about 20 minutes.

Check the potatoes by piercing the center of one with the tip of a small, sharp knife—it should go in easily with just a little resistance (you'll be cooking the potatoes again). Drain and leave to cool.

Cut each potato in half, then slice any large ones into ½in (1cm) thick disks. Heat the oil in a large, non-stick skillet over medium-high heat until it gives off a light haze. Place the potatoes in the pan, spread them out, and season with fine salt. Sauté for 3–6 minutes until golden brown underneath. Turn the slices over with a metal spatula, season with salt again, and cook for 2–3 minutes longer until the second side is golden brown.

Add the butter and melt it. Shake the pan to coat the potatoes with hot butter, then remove them from the pan with a spatula and drain briefly on paper towels. Season with sea salt and serve hot.

KEY TO PERFECTION

Sautéed potatoes should be crisp, with a nutty color and flavor. The way to achieve this is by adding cold butter to the hot oil at the end.

Once the potatoes are crisp on both sides, dot the cubes of butter in between the slices, spacing the butter evenly in the pan.

Shake the pan and watch the butter foam up, then wait a minute or two until it goes nutty brown (*noisette*). Remove from the heat immediately, before it overheats and turns dark.

SPINACH WITH GARLIC AND CREAM

Just as tomatoes go with basil and olive oil, spinach is good with garlic, nutmeg, and cream. For me they are a perfect combination. This dish is a great accompaniment for pan-grilled meat, particularly lamb.

SERVES 2

1lb 2oz (500g) baby spinach leaves
1 cup heavy cream
freshly grated nutmeg
1 plump garlic clove, peeled and cut lengthwise into thirds
2 tbsp olive oil
sea salt and freshly milled black pepper

Even though spinach in bags is sold as washed, it's always a good idea to wash it yourself to be sure there's no grit lurking in the leaves. Immerse the leaves in the sink or a large bowl filled with cold water, and swish it around for a minute or so. Drain in a colander, then turn it out onto a cloth or paper towels and gently pat dry. If you notice any stems that are particularly coarse, snap them off.

Put the cream in a heavy saucepan with a few gratings of nutmeg and a pinch of salt. Simmer for 8–10 minutes, stirring often, until you have about 4 tbsp left in the bottom of the pan. Remove from the heat.

Spear the garlic onto a fork. Spoon the oil into a wok or a large, deep skillet and put over high heat. When the oil is hot, toss in the spinach leaves and season lightly with salt, then stir with the garlic fork until the spinach has wilted.

Transfer the contents of the pan to a colander and press the spinach with the garlic fork to get rid of excess water. Put the spinach back into the pan and reheat, shaking the pan constantly.

Pour the reduced cream over the spinach and stir with the garlic fork until all the leaves are coated with cream. Check the seasoning, then serve the spinach hot.

"Freshly grated nutmeg is always better than ground, but be careful how much you use, as too much can be overpowering."

KEY TO PERFECTION

Although spinach and garlic go really well together, not everyone likes eating pieces of garlic, even when they're finely chopped or crushed. The way to get the flavor without the bits is to use a "garlic fork."

Swish the garlic fork back and forth through the spinach during cooking, shaking the pan at the same time.

Skewer the pieces of garlic firmly onto the tines of a fork, securing them by pushing them down as far as they will go without breaking.

ALL IS NOT LOST

If the dish looks too watery at the end, lift the spinach out with a slotted spoon and drain in a colander set over a bowl. Add the drained liquid to the creamy liquid left in the pan and boil until reduced, then return the spinach to the pan and toss until hot.

BROCCOLI AND GREEN BEAN SAUTÉ

Adding crunchy cashews and fresh almonds to broccoli and green beans is a really great way of serving these two simple vegetables. It makes you want to eat them all on their own.

SERVES 4

1 large head of broccoli, cut into
   small florets, with stems
   trimmed on the diagonal
8oz (225g) green beans,
   preferably thin haricots
   verts, tops trimmed but
   not the curved tails
3 tbsp olive oil, plus extra
   for drizzling
about 10 unsalted cashew nuts,
   halved lengthwise
about 10 freshly blanched
   almonds, halved lengthwise
sea salt

Fill a large bowl half full with cold water and drop in a few handfuls of ice cubes. Set aside.

Plunge the broccoli florets into a large pan of salted boiling water, bring the water back to a boil, and simmer for 1 minute. Drain and refresh in the ice water. Repeat with the beans, then drain both vegetables and dry them on a cloth.

Put the oil in a wok or large, non-stick skillet and set over high heat. When you can just see a haze rising, add the cashews and toss until browned. Add the broccoli and sauté for 2 minutes before tossing in the beans. Sauté for another 2 minutes. Remove from the heat and toss in the almonds.

Sprinkle with sea salt, drizzle with olive oil, and serve.

"Fresh almonds are stronger in flavor than dried. If you can't get them, use dried almonds or sliced canned water chestnuts instead. Nuts have a short shelf life, so always buy them from a shop with a fast turnover."

KEY TO PERFECTION

Green vegetables benefit from being blanched in boiling water before sautéing, so they will cook quickly in the hot oil and not get too brown. The secret of keeping their bright color is to "refresh" them in ice water immediately after blanching. This stops the cooking and sets the color.

Plunge the hot, drained vegetables into the bowl of ice water. Leave until they are cold, then drain. The color will stay bright green.

ONE-POT ROASTED VEGETABLES

I created this easy side dish when we had friends coming over one Sunday. I didn't want to spend a lot of time in the kitchen while they were there, so before they arrived I put the roast in the oven in one roasting pan and the vegetables in another. As a result, I had very little work to do until just before serving time.

SERVES 4

²/₃ cup vegetable oil

3 parsnips, peeled and cut into
   2in (5cm) pieces

1 celeriac (also called celery
   root), weighing about 14oz
   (400g), peeled and cut into
   2in (5cm) pieces

1lb 2oz (500g) baby red-skinned
   potatoes, washed and left
   whole, or halved if large

4 carrots, peeled and cut into
   2in (5cm) pieces on the diagonal

2–3 celery ribs, strings removed
   and cut into 2in (5cm) pieces
   on the diagonal

12 Italian cipolline or shallots,
   quartered lengthwise

1 bulb garlic, broken open without
   peeling the cloves

1–2 lemons, preferably organic,
   cut lengthwise into wedges

5 sprigs of fresh rosemary

10 sprigs of fresh thyme

4 bay leaves

sea salt and freshly milled
   black pepper

Preheat the oven to 425°F (220°C).

Put the oil in a large, heavy roasting pan and heat in the oven for about 5 minutes until a light haze rises off the oil. Carefully add all the vegetables, the garlic, lemon wedges, and herbs to the hot oil. Season, and stir well to mix.

Return the pan to the oven and roast for 50 minutes to 1 hour, stirring every 20 minutes, until the vegetables are tender and tinged with brown. Serve immediately.

"Cipolline are small, flat Italian onions. I particularly like their sweet flavor with the other vegetables in this dish, but you can use shallots instead."

KEY TO PERFECTION

To be sure all the different vegetables cook in the same amount of time, they must be cut into similar-sized pieces. Some are easier to deal with than others.

Celeriac is unwieldy to prepare because it's so hard and knobby, but it's well worth including for its nutty flavor. After peeling it thickly and trimming off the ends, cut it vertically into quarters. Now you'll find it easy to cut the quarters into neat pieces.

Parsnips need special attention because they often have tough, woody cores, especially if they are large or old. Before cutting them into pieces, quarter them lengthwise and cut off the hard ridge running down the inside edge of each piece.

Although the vegetables start off completely different in shape and size, when cut into uniform shapes they'll become tender at the same time.

BITTERSWEET GREENS SALAD

With its contrast of bitter and sweet, as well as crisp and tender, this is a sensational salad. I love the taste of the bitter leaves tossed in a mustard vinaigrette, combined with a sharp, crisp apple to add its lovely sweet and sour flavor.

SERVES 4
1 head of radicchio
1 head of Belgian endive
1 head of frisée
5 sprigs of fresh cilantro
2 Granny Smith apples
4 tbsp Vinaigrette Dressing
   (below)

Separate the radicchio and endive leaves and cut them lengthwise in half if they are large. Separate the frisée leaves; use only the lightest leaves from the center. Pick the leaves off the cilantro stems. Rinse all the leaves in cold water, drain them in a colander, and dry well by shaking in a cloth.

Peel, quarter, and core the apples. Cut the quarters into thin slices and then into matchsticks.

Mix the leaves and apples together in a large bowl.

Pour the dressing over the salad in the bowl and toss gently with your hands until all the leaves are coated. Serve immediately.

VINAIGRETTE DRESSING

MAKES ABOUT 1¼ CUPS
1 heaped tbsp Dijon mustard
about 4 tbsp white wine vinegar
1 cup extra-virgin olive oil
sea salt and freshly milled
   black pepper

Whisk the mustard with a large pinch each of salt and pepper. Whisk in 2 tbsp vinegar, then gradually whisk in the oil. Taste and add more vinegar and seasoning if you like. Keep in a tightly covered jar in the refrigerator. Before use, shake well to emulsify the dressing again, then taste and correct the seasoning if necessary.

KEY TO PERFECTION

Fresh salad leaves need a good dressing to bring out their flavor. Vinaigrette is the classic oil and vinegar combination, and the ratio of one to another is as important as the way they are mixed. I use five parts oil to one part vinegar, which is rather more oil than in most recipes, but to me it's the perfect balance—any more vinegar and it would kill off the taste of the leaves.

After mixing the mustard and seasonings to make a thick base, the oil will quickly emulsify when you whisk it in. Add it slowly in a thin, steady stream, whisking vigorously.

When all the oil has been incorporated, the dressing will be beautifully creamy and thick.

Use your hands to gently toss the salad leaves and dressing together. This way you can be sure all the leaves are lightly and evenly coated, and the leaves will not be bruised.

GREEN SALAD WITH HERBS

Try to get as much variety as possible in your leafy salads, both for looks and for flavor. Rather than using a prepared mesclun mixture from the produce market, simply buy what looks freshest on the day. This way you'll have a different salad every time.

SERVES 4–6

2oz (50g) baby arugula leaves
1oz (25g) Lollo Rosso leaves
1oz (25g) baby red chard leaves
1 head of frisée, light green leaves only
1 bunch of watercress, leaves only
5 tbsp pea shoots (optional)
5 tbsp fresh chervil leaves
5 tbsp fresh cilantro leaves
2 tbsp fresh tarragon leaves
about 24 fresh basil leaves, torn
4–5 tbsp Vinaigrette Dressing (page 114)
sea salt and freshly milled black pepper

Rinse, drain, and dry all the salad and herb leaves. Put them in a large bowl.

Add the dressing and toss gently with your hands until all the leaves are evenly coated with dressing.

Pile the salad in individual bowls or on plates and serve immediately.

KEY TO PERFECTION

The leaves must be thoroughly dry. If they are wet, the dressing won't cling to them and the salad will be watery and insipid.

After rinsing the leaves under cold water, shake and turn them in a colander to remove excess water.

Remove the leaves from the colander, then line it with a towel. Drop in a handful of leaves, bring the ends up to form a loose bundle, and shake gently to get the leaves as dry as possible. Repeat with the rest of the leaves.

"Salad leaves are delicate and should be handled with care.
Don't use a salad spinner for drying because it will bruise them."

TOMATO SALAD WITH SHALLOTS

There is nothing more refreshing than a chilled tomato salad, especially during their peak summer season. If you cut the tomatoes into smaller pieces, you'll have a salsa to serve with grilled chicken or steak.

SERVES 4
1–1¼lb (500–600g) ripe tomatoes, hulls removed
8 ripe cherry tomatoes on the vine
3–4 shallots, finely sliced into rings
a few sprigs each of fresh basil and cilantro
a handful of baby arugula leaves
4 tbsp Vinaigrette Dressing (page 114)
sea salt and freshly milled black pepper

Blanch, refresh, and drain the large tomatoes (not the cherry tomatoes). Peel and quarter them, then put them in a bowl.

Snip the cherry tomatoes off the vine into the bowl and add the shallots. Pick the basil and cilantro leaves off the stems and drop into the bowl. Add the arugula, then drizzle the dressing over and toss gently to mix. Cover and refrigerate for a couple of hours.

Before serving, taste and correct the seasoning if necessary.

"If the tomatoes are peeled, the dressing can draw out their juices as if making them bleed, and this accentuates their flavor."

KEY TO PERFECTION

If you are lucky enough to get locally grown tomatoes in the summer you can eat them as they are. At other times of the year, tomato skins can be tough, and will spoil an otherwise good tomato salad, so it is best to peel them.

With a sharp knife, make a shallow, cross-shaped incision in the rounded end of each tomato. This will help loosen the skin during blanching.

Blanch the tomatoes by immersing them in a pan of boiling water for 10–30 seconds until you see the skins start to split.

Lift the tomatoes out of the hot water with a slotted spoon as soon as the skins split, then plunge immediately into ice water. Leave to cool for 5 minutes, then remove and drain on a cloth or paper towels.

Peel off the skins with a small, sharp knife—they will come away easily.

SWEET PEPPER SALAD

This salad is great served warm with grilled fish or burgers, and is equally good chilled or at room temperature as a relish with cheese. Use red and yellow bell peppers, but not green ones.

SERVES 4
½ cup olive oil
4 red bell peppers
4 yellow bell peppers
10–12 sprigs of fresh thyme
2 red onions, thinly sliced
4 garlic cloves, thinly sliced
a handful of fresh basil leaves, thinly sliced
a handful of fresh marjoram leaves
sea salt and freshly milled black pepper

Preheat the oven to 425°F (220°C).

Put 3 tbsp of the oil in a heavy flameproof roasting pan and place over high heat. When hot, add the whole peppers, a few thyme sprigs, and salt and pepper. Fry for about 10 minutes until the peppers are tinged brown on all sides. Transfer the pan to the oven and roast the peppers for 10 minutes until softened. Immediately put the peppers in a large bowl and cover tightly with plastic wrap. Let cool.

Peel the skin off the peppers. Cut each pepper in half lengthwise and cut off the stem end, then scrape out the seeds and ribs from inside. Slice the flesh lengthwise into ¼in (5mm) wide strips. Reserve the pepper juices.

Heat 2 tbsp oil in a skillet over medium heat until hot. Add the onions with the garlic and the remaining thyme and sauté for a few minutes. Season with salt, then cook until the onions are lightly colored and softening. Remove the thyme. Add the peppers and seasoning and cook for 2 minutes longer. Transfer to a bowl, add the reserved pepper juices, and leave to cool a little.

To serve, stir the basil and marjoram through the peppers, drizzle with the remaining oil, and sprinkle with sea salt.

"To keep these peppers as a relish, add a few spoonfuls of wine vinegar and store in a tightly sealed jar in the refrigerator."

KEY TO PERFECTION

Pepper skin is tough, so it's best to peel peppers for a salad. Many recipes suggest charring the skin over a gas flame to loosen it, but this can make the peppers taste bitter. A combination of frying and roasting gives a sweeter result.

When frying the peppers, let them sit undisturbed until the skin colors and starts to blister underneath before turning them and browning the next side.

Cool the fried and roasted peppers in a bowl sealed with plastic wrap. The steam inside will loosen the skins and make the peppers juicy. Wait until they are cold before removing the wrap.

Peel off the skin with a small knife—it will come away easily. Have a bowl of warm water handy, so you can keep dipping the knife in to keep it clean.

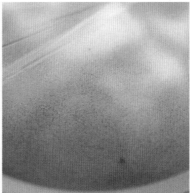

Once they are peeled, the peppers will be silky smooth and ready to slice into neat strips for the salad.

PASTA, LEGUMES & GRAINS

BAKED PENNE WITH BOLOGNESE

Although there are many contenders for the crown, bolognese is probably the king of pasta sauces. It's often tossed with pasta and sprinkled with freshly grated Parmesan, but here's a baked version with creamy Taleggio cheese. This is a great dish to feed a crowd, because it can be prepared ahead and cooked when you need it.

SERVES 6

2 tsp fine table salt
1lb 2oz (500g) dried penne rigate
   or plain penne
olive oil
1lb 2oz (500g) Taleggio cheese,
   thinly sliced
2 tbsp chopped fresh flat-leaf
   parsley, to finish

FOR THE BOLOGNESE SAUCE

3 tbsp olive oil
4 tbsp (¹/₂ stick) unsalted butter
1 large yellow onion,
   finely chopped
4 celery ribs, strings removed
   and finely chopped
2 carrots, peeled and
   finely chopped
3 garlic cloves, finely chopped
4 sprigs of fresh thyme
4 sprigs of fresh marjoram
2 bay leaves
1lb 2oz (500g) lean ground beef,
   such as sirloin or round
2 tbsp tomato paste
10 ripe plum or roma tomatoes,
   peeled (page 119), deseeded,
   and chopped, or 14oz (400g)
   can crushed tomatoes
sea salt and freshly milled
   black pepper

First make the bolognese sauce. Heat the oil and butter in a large, heavy pan over medium heat. Add the onion, celery, carrots, garlic, and herbs, and cook until the vegetables are light golden brown. Add the ground beef and cook until it starts to color, stirring to break up any lumps. Season and stir in the tomato paste. Cook for 5 minutes longer, then stir in the tomatoes and 1 cup water. Cover and cook over low heat for 1 hour, stirring occasionally.

Bring a large pot of water to a rapid boil over high heat. Add the salt, then the pasta, and stir well. Cover the pan and bring the water back to a boil, then take the lid off and turn the heat down slightly. Boil for 10–12 minutes, or according to package directions, stirring frequently, until the pasta is *al dente* (tender, but still with a little bite).

Preheat the oven to 375°F (190°C).

Drain the pasta well in a colander, then transfer to a very large bowl. Pour the sauce into the bowl and mix well, moistening with a splash of olive oil. Taste for seasoning. Transfer to a large baking dish and lay the slices of Taleggio on top, overlapping them slightly. Bake for 30 minutes until the cheese is golden brown and bubbling. Serve hot, sprinkled with chopped parsley and black pepper.

KEY TO PERFECTION

You can cook pasta following the directions on the package, but there are a couple of things they won't tell you that can make a big difference to the success of the finished dish—adding the pasta to water that is boiling rapidly and then keeping it on the move.

The water should be at a rolling boil when the pasta goes in, so it will start cooking immediately and you can time it accurately. To make sure of this, bring the water to a boil and throw in the salt, then watch the water surge. This is your cue to put in the pasta.

After the water has returned to a boil, remove the lid, then stir the pasta frequently during cooking to prevent the pieces from clumping together.

LINGUINE WITH PESTO

Although you can make pesto well ahead of serving and store it in a tightly covered container in the refrigerator, it is fantastic if it's freshly made and eaten right away. The color and flavor of homemade pesto are incredibly intense—totally different from store-bought pesto.

SERVES 4–6
2 tsp fine table salt
1lb 2oz (500g) dried linguine
extra-virgin olive oil, for drizzling
grated fresh Parmesan cheese,
    to serve

FOR THE PESTO
leaves of 1 large bunch of fresh
    basil, weighing about 2¹⁄₂oz
    (65g), about 2 packed cups
¹⁄₃ cup pine nuts, toasted in
    a skillet until golden brown
1 garlic clove, finely chopped
¹⁄₃ cup freshly grated Parmesan
    cheese
1 cup extra-virgin olive oil
sea salt and freshly milled
    black pepper

Bring a large pot of water to a rapid boil over high heat. Add the fine salt, immediately coil the pasta into the water, and cover the pan. Bring the water back to a boil, then take the lid off the pan and turn the heat down slightly. Boil for 10–12 minutes, or according to package directions, stirring frequently, until the pasta is *al dente* (tender, but still with a little bite).

Make the pesto while the pasta is cooking. Pulse the basil leaves with the pine nuts, garlic, Parmesan, and seasoning in the blender a few times, then pulse in the oil, drizzling it through the hole in the lid. Stop occasionally to scrape down the sides.

Drain the pasta well in a colander, then transfer it to a large bowl. Drizzle with a splash of olive oil and toss to keep the strands separate, then add the pesto and toss again until the pasta is evenly coated.

Divide among warmed bowls, drizzle with olive oil, and top with grated Parmesan. Serve immediately.

KEY TO PERFECTION

Basil is one of the most delicate herbs. It bruises easily, and quickly loses aroma and flavor once it's cut, so for the brightest color and freshest taste, the less it's chopped the better. This is why pesto should be made quickly, have a rough and ready texture, and be eaten as soon as possible after it's made.

Pick the basil leaves off their stems and drop them into the blender. Add the remaining pesto ingredients, except the oil, then pulse a few times—just until roughly chopped.

Work the oil into the pesto with the blender on pulse. Check how it's doing after every pulse or two, and stop while it's still chunky. Don't grind it to a purée—you should see flecks of pine nuts throughout the pesto.

As soon as you've drained the pasta and tossed it with a little olive oil, pour the freshly made pesto onto it, straight from the blender. Scrape the inside so none of the pesto is wasted.

TAGLIATELLE WITH CRAB

A delicately flavored seafood sauce such as this one goes best with fresh, handmade pasta. I always make more pasta dough than I need because I find it works better with a large quantity of flour and eggs. Leftover dough will keep in the refrigerator for a couple of days.

SERVES 4

½ quantity fresh Pasta Dough
  (opposite)
2 tbsp olive oil, plus extra
  for drizzling
2 shallots, minced
2 garlic cloves, finely sliced
2 plump, hot red chilies,
  deseeded and minced
12oz (350g) fresh white crab
  meat, picked over to remove
  all shells and cartilage
5–6 tbsp minced fresh
  flat-leaf parsley
2 tsp fine table salt
sea salt and freshly milled
  black pepper

Divide the pasta dough in half. On a floured surface, roll out each piece into a strip that is roughly the same width as your pasta machine. Sprinkle the strips with flour and crank each one through the machine until the dough is very smooth, thin, and even. Machines vary, but most require the dough to be cranked through many times, working down from the highest notch to the lowest with each rolling, sprinkling with flour in between. When the strips get too long to handle, cut them into two short lengths before the next rolling. If the pasta looks too coarse at the end, fold the strips in fourths and crank them through again, from the highest notch down to the lowest.

Cut the pasta into tagliatelle with the machine, then hang the pasta ribbons on a floured, clean broom handle set across the back of two chairs.

Heat the oil in a non-stick skillet over low to medium heat. Add the shallots, garlic, and chilies with salt and pepper to taste and fry until soft. Gently fold in the crab meat and parsley. Remove from the heat and keep warm.

Bring a large pot of water to a rapid boil over high heat. Add the fine salt, then immediately drop in the pasta, give it a quick stir, and cover the pan. Bring the water back to a boil. Take the lid off the pan and turn the heat down a little. Boil the tagliatelle for 2–3 minutes, stirring occasionally, until it is tender.

Drain the tagliatelle well in a colander, then transfer to a large bowl. Drizzle with olive oil and toss gently to coat the strands, then add the crab mixture and toss gently again until all the pasta is evenly coated. Serve immediately, with more olive oil for drizzling if you like.

PASTA DOUGH

MAKES ABOUT 2LB (900G)
2 cups all-purpose flour
2 cups cake flour (not self-rising)
1 tsp fine table salt
4 extra large eggs, preferably organic
6 extra large egg yolks, preferably organic
2 tbsp olive oil

Put the flours and salt into a food processor fitted with the metal chopping blade. Beat the eggs and egg yolks together in a pitcher, then pour about one-third into the machine and pulse to mix. With the machine running, add the oil and more of the eggs through the funnel. You'll need only enough egg to make the mixture look crumbly. Don't overwork it. Turn out onto a floured surface and knead until smooth. Wrap in plastic wrap and refrigerate for at least 1 hour before using.

KEY TO PERFECTION

Making your own pasta dough is easy. This recipe has a large quantity of eggs and egg yolks, which produces a very rich and silky pasta.

After doing the squeeze test, don't worry when the mix turns out of the machine like a messy crumble. It will soon come together when you start kneading.

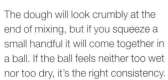

The dough will look crumbly at the end of mixing, but if you squeeze a small handful it will come together in a ball. If the ball feels neither too wet nor too dry, it's the right consistency.

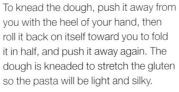

To knead the dough, push it away from you with the heel of your hand, then roll it back on itself toward you to fold it in half, and push it away again. The dough is kneaded to stretch the gluten so the pasta will be light and silky.

Stop kneading when the dough is smooth. It should be dull, not shiny. Form into a ball, wrap in plastic wrap, and let it relax in the refrigerator for at least an hour. Don't skip this stage or the dough will be too springy to roll.

EGG FRIED RICE

A Chinese restaurant in England was where I had my first taste of
"foreign" cuisine. I ordered egg fried rice—it seemed to be the most
familiar dish on the menu. Even though I gradually got braver and
started eating more adventurous things, it's still one of my favorites.

SERVES 4
2½ cups long-grain rice
pinch of fine table salt
2 tbsp vegetable oil
4 extra large eggs, preferably
   organic, beaten
soy sauce, to taste

Wash, drain, and rinse the rice until the water is clear.

Fill a large saucepan with water, bring to a boil, and add the salt.
The large amount of water is important—it helps to dilute the starch,
like the washing and rinsing, and to keep the grains of rice separate.

Add the rice to the water, stir, and boil uncovered over high heat
for 10–12 minutes until the rice is tender. Drain in a sieve, rinse, and
pat dry, then leave to dry out and cool for about half an hour.

Place a non-stick wok or large, deep skillet over high heat.
When hot, add the oil and heat until you can see a light haze rising.
Pour in the eggs, and cook and stir until lightly scrambled.

Pour in the rice. Stir and toss the rice and eggs together until the
rice is piping hot and the eggs are evenly mixed through, then sprinkle
with soy sauce to taste. Toss to mix and serve immediately.

*"If you add a lot of salt to the water when
boiling rice it can rupture the grains and
make them stick together. For this reason,
only add the smallest amount of salt—
just enough to bring out the flavor."*

KEY TO PERFECTION

Rice tends to stick when it's being fried, even in a non-stick pan. To prevent this from happening, you need to get rid of as much starch as possible from the rice before you start frying, and the rice must be cold and dry.

Before boiling the rice, put it in a large bowl and fill two-thirds full with cold water, then swish it around with your fingers to release the starch. The water will turn cloudy and milky white. Pour the rice into a large sieve and let the water drain through, then rinse the rice under cold water.

Put the rice back in the rinsed-out bowl, fill with fresh cold water as before, and swish again. This time the water will be less cloudy. Drain and rinse the rice, and repeat until the water remains clear.

When the rice has boiled until tender, drain it in a large sieve. Hold under cold water to stop the cooking, shaking the sieve to make sure every grain of rice gets rinsed. The longer you rinse the better, as this will wash off the last of the starch. Now pour the rice onto a baking sheet, spread it out, and pat off the excess moisture with a clean cloth or paper towels.

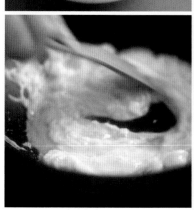

Cooking the eggs first will also help to prevent the rice from sticking to the pan. Add the beaten eggs to the hot oil and tilt the pan from side to side so the eggs cover the bottom, then quickly stir with a wooden spatula for a couple of minutes until the eggs are lightly scrambled.

RISOTTO

This is a calming, effortless dish. I just love to stand stirring at the stove, at one with my risotto—and a glass of chilled dry white wine. You have to open a bottle for cooking, after all.

SERVES 4

about 5½ cups hot Chicken Stock (page 16)
1 sprig of fresh thyme
3 tbsp olive oil
2 shallots, finely chopped
1 small garlic clove, finely chopped
2½ cups Carnaroli or Vialone Nano rice
a good splash of dry white wine (about ½ cup)
sea salt and freshly milled black pepper

TO FINISH

about 2oz (50g) fresh Parmesan cheese (⅓ cup grated and the rest shaved), plus more to taste
4 tbsp (½ stick) cold unsalted butter, diced
4 tbsp mascarpone

Put the stock and thyme in a pan and bring to a boil, then leave at a gentle simmer on the stove.

Heat the oil in a large, deep, heavy saucepan over medium heat. Add the shallots and garlic, and cook for a few minutes without coloring until they start to soften.

Pour in the rice, and stir and cook for a few minutes until it becomes shiny and translucent. Now listen for a popping sound—this is the sign that the rice is ready for the liquid to be added. Splash in the wine and let it reduce to nothing, stirring constantly.

Add a ladleful of the hot stock, season, and stir. Simmer, stirring, until you can no longer see the stock, then add the rest of the stock a ladleful at a time, stirring constantly until each has been absorbed before adding the next. The total cooking time for the risotto should be 15–20 minutes.

To check if the risotto is done, shake the pan and toss the rice. If it's loose enough to find its own way around the pan, it's ready. If not, add a little more stock and continue to cook until you are happy with the consistency. Another way to check is to taste a few grains of rice. If there's a chalky crunch on the outside, cook for a few more minutes. Use a little boiling water if you are totally out of stock.

To finish, stir in the grated Parmesan, then the butter two pieces at a time, and finally the mascarpone. Taste for seasoning and add more grated Parmesan if you like. Serve in wide, shallow bowls topped with the shaved Parmesan.

"Mascarpone isn't a classic ingredient in risotto, and it's not essential to include it in this recipe, but it does make the rice very rich and creamy, which is how I like it."

KEY TO PERFECTION

A perfectly cooked risotto should be creamy in consistency, not sloppy or mushy, and the grains of rice should retain some bite. Get the stock hot and all the other ingredients prepared in advance, and stand over the pan the whole time the risotto is cooking. Don't walk away from it, not even for a minute.

At the beginning, get the flavor base of shallots and garlic nice and soft before adding the rice to the pot all at once. Stir immediately to coat the rice in the oil and shallots.

After cooking the rice until it is translucent, and reducing the wine until it's all gone, you will be able to draw a path through the rice with the spatula. Now you can start adding the hot chicken stock.

The stock must be added in small batches —wait until each batch is absorbed before adding the next—while stirring constantly. Stirring keeps the rice active and moving, which releases the starch from the grains to make the risotto creamy.

ALL IS NOT LOST

If you've overcooked the rice (or you've got some risotto left over), refrigerate until firm, then shape into balls or flat cakes. Coat in flour, then in beaten egg and bread crumbs, and fry in olive oil until golden and crisp.

BE PREPARED

"Before starting to cook, measure ingredients and complete any preparation steps like peeling, slicing, and chopping."

COUSCOUS WITH CANDIED LEMON

I discovered candied lemon when I worked in New York with Daniel Boulud. It isn't a confection, but a wonderful sweet-sour garnish that adds a special Middle Eastern flavor to all kinds of dishes. I love it in this couscous side dish, which is perfect with pan-grilled duck breasts.

SERVES 4

1¼ cups fine couscous
1 cup hot Chicken Stock
   (page 16)
½ cup raisins
½ cup shelled pistachio nuts,
   toasted in a skillet and
   roughly chopped
a handful of fresh cilantro
   leaves, chopped
a splash of Vinaigrette Dressing
   (page 114)

FOR THE CANDIED LEMON

¾ cup granulated sugar
1 small lemon, preferably
   organic, very thinly sliced
   and seeds removed

First candy the lemon. Mix the sugar with ⅔ cup cold water in a heavy saucepan and bring to a boil over medium heat. Add the lemon slices. Reduce the heat so the liquid is barely simmering and cook for 40 minutes to 1 hour until the slices are soft and syrupy.

Meanwhile, put the couscous in a large bowl and whisk in the stock. Cover tightly with plastic wrap and leave in a warm place for at least 30 minutes, whisking several times. Put the raisins in a small bowl, cover with warm water, and leave to soak.

Remove the lemon slices from the syrup. When cool enough to handle, chop into small pieces. Drain the raisins and chop roughly.

Fluff up the couscous. Add about one-third of the chopped lemon along with the raisins and pistachios, and mix well. Serve at room temperature, or warm through in a bowl set over a pan of simmering water for a few minutes. Before serving, stir in the cilantro and dressing, then check the seasoning and add more candied lemon if you like.

KEY TO PERFECTION

Couscous should be light and fluffy, with individual grains that have a nutty texture when you bite into them. There should be no lumps or clumps of couscous stuck together.

As you pour in the hot stock, whisk constantly to separate the couscous grains. They will then be free to absorb the stock during standing.

At the end of soaking, the couscous will have increased in volume and the grains will be swollen and plump. Stroke through them with a fork, and separate any clumps with your fingers.

CHILI BEANS

Chili used to mean just one thing—a big pot of spicy beef and beans —but now you can make chili with a wide range of ingredients, from chicken to seafood. This is a vegetarian version I devised when I was working in upstate New York. It uses an interesting mix of legumes.

SERVES 4–6

½ cup dried red kidney beans,
   soaked in cold water
   overnight and drained
½ cup dried green adzuki beans,
   soaked in cold water for
   a few hours and drained
⅓ cup Puy lentils
5 tbsp olive oil
1 yellow onion, finely chopped
2 red bell peppers, finely chopped
2 hot red chilies, deseeded and
   finely chopped
2 garlic cloves, finely chopped
2 tsp chili powder (medium or
   hot, to taste)
11oz (300g) ripe tomatoes,
   peeled (page 119), deseeded,
   and chopped, or 14oz (400g)
   can crushed tomatoes
2 cups tomato juice
leaves of 1 small bunch of fresh
   cilantro, roughly chopped
sea salt and freshly milled
   black pepper

Blanch, drain, and rinse the kidney beans, then return them to the rinsed-out pan and cover generously with fresh cold water. Bring to a boil over high heat again, and boil rapidly without the lid for 10 minutes. Half cover the pan, turn down the heat, and simmer the beans for 30–45 minutes until tender.

Meanwhile, blanch the adzuki beans and lentils as you did for the kidney beans, using a separate pan for each. Drain and rinse, then bring both to a boil in separate pans of water. Half cover the pans and simmer until tender, allowing 12–15 minutes for the adzuki beans, 20–25 minutes for the lentils. Drain the kidney and adzuki beans and the lentils, and set aside.

Heat the olive oil in a heavy saucepan over medium heat and add the onion, red peppers, chilies, and garlic. Sprinkle in the chili powder and a pinch of salt. Cook for 5 minutes until the vegetables are softened, stirring occasionally. Add the tomatoes followed by the beans, lentils, and tomato juice, and stir well to mix. Cover and simmer over low heat for 45 minutes to 1 hour, stirring occasionally, until the sauce has thickened.

Stir some of the cilantro into the beans and add seasoning to taste. Serve with the remaining cilantro sprinkled on top.

"If you are short on time, use canned beans and lentils —you can use any type of beans you like."

KEY TO PERFECTION

To help make red kidney beans easier to digest by reducing their gassy effect, and to get rid of any toxins, blanch and boil them rapidly before leaving them to cook.

At the start of cooking, rapidly boil the beans for 10 minutes. This will destroy any toxins that red kidney beans may contain. With a ladle, scoop off the scum as it rises to the surface during this time—this will keep the water clear.

To blanch the beans, put them in a saucepan of cold water and bring to a boil over high heat. Drain immediately in a colander, hold the colander under cold water, and rinse the beans thoroughly to wash off all the scum.

ALL IS NOT LOST

If the chili beans get overcooked and turn mushy, just strain off the excess liquid by pouring the beans into a sieve, then purée them in a blender or food processor. Chill and serve as a dip, topped with a few whole beans, some chopped fresh cilantro, and a sprinkling of paprika and olive oil.

LENTILS WITH HERBS

Don't push legumes to the back of the cupboard—they deserve better treatment. When you make an effort and add interesting things to them, you'll be amazed how good they are—and they're good for you too. It's time they lost their boring image.

SERVES 4
3/4 cup Puy lentils
2 cups Vegetable Nage (page 22)
2 small carrots, peeled and
    halved lengthwise
1 onion, cut lengthwise into
    chunks
1 small leek, cut into chunks
1 celery rib, strings removed and
    cut crosswise in half
1 sprig of fresh thyme

FOR THE SECOND STAGE
3 shallots, minced
1/2 celery rib, strings removed
    and minced
1/2 carrot, peeled and minced
4–7 tbsp (1/2 stick plus up to
    3 tbsp) cold unsalted
    butter, diced
about 3 tbsp finely chopped
    fresh herbs (parsley, chervil,
    and chives)
sea salt and freshly milled
    black pepper

Rinse the lentils in a sieve under cold water, pour into a saucepan, and cover generously with cold water. Bring to a boil, then drain in the sieve and rinse well again.

Return the lentils to the rinsed-out pan and pour in half the nage and 1 cup cold water. Add the carrots, onion, leek, celery, and thyme. Stir, then cover closely with a piece of parchment paper. Bring to a boil. Turn the heat down and simmer gently for 5–8 minutes until the lentils are half cooked. Drain in a sieve; discard the vegetables and thyme.

For the second stage, return the lentils to the rinsed-out pan and pour in the remaining nage. Add the minced shallots, celery, and carrot, and bring to a boil over medium to high heat. Reduce the heat and simmer gently, uncovered, for about 10 minutes until there is half as much liquid as lentils.

Add as much butter as you like, a little at a time, stirring until it is all incorporated—the end result should be a shiny emulsion. Stir in the chopped herbs, season, and serve.

KEY TO PERFECTION

Unlike dried beans, lentils don't need soaking and they cook very quickly, but they should be blanched before they're cooked with other ingredients. If you don't do this, the finished dish will be murky and gray.

Blanch the lentils by putting them in a pan of cold water and bringing them to a boil. Drain in a sieve and rinse well under cold water to wash away all the discolored lentil water.

When the lentils have been blanched, they will readily absorb the flavors of the chunky vegetables and fresh thyme sprigs.

EGGS

SCRAMBLED EGGS

We often have scrambled eggs at home on Sunday mornings—the boys like their eggs on buttered biscuits rather than toast. While everyone knows how to make scrambled eggs, the tips here will ensure a perfect creamy result every time.

SERVES 2
6 extra large eggs, preferably
   organic
2 tbsp heavy cream
a splash of milk
4 tbsp (¹/₂ stick) unsalted
   butter, diced
sea salt and freshly milled
   black pepper
buttered toasted English
   muffins or crumpets, to serve
snipped fresh chives,
   for garnish

Lightly whisk the eggs with the cream and milk in a bowl, and season with a little salt.

Put a large, non-stick skillet over low heat until hot. Add the butter and heat until foaming, then pour in the eggs and move them slowly around the bottom and side of the pan. Keep them moving like this for 2–3 minutes until the eggs look soft and creamy.

Immediately remove the pan from the heat and spoon the eggs onto the hot buttered muffins or crumpets. Sprinkle with snipped chives and black pepper, and serve immediately.

KEY TO PERFECTION

For soft and creamy scrambled eggs, you need to know exactly when to start cooking—and when to stop. Even over low heat, the eggs will be done sooner than you think.

 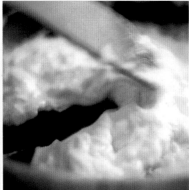

While the eggs are slowly scrambling, keep them on the move. Scrape them constantly off the bottom and side of the pan with a flat wooden spatula (this will get into the edge of the pan better than a spoon), and be ready to whip the pan off the heat when the first large "curds" appear. The eggs will continue to cook in their own heat after they've been taken off the stove, so it's vital to stop cooking at this point or they'll become rubbery and watery.

Get the butter hot and foaming before you pour in the eggs. The heat of the butter will then start cooking the eggs the second they run over the bottom of the pan.

FRIED EGGS BANJO

I got the name "banjo" from my grandfather. It's an old Army term for a fried egg sandwich made with stale bread, margarine, and ketchup. This is my version, using slightly better ingredients!

SERVES 2
1 small, flat loaf of country
   bread
olive oil, for drizzling
4 tbsp (½ stick) cold unsalted
   butter, cut into 8 cubes
4 extra large eggs, preferably
   organic
tomato ketchup
sea salt and freshly milled
   black pepper

Cut the loaf in half through the middle, as if making a large sandwich. Heat a ridged grill pan until it is very hot. Drizzle olive oil over the cut sides of the loaf and rub it in, then chargrill the halves cut-side down on the hot grill pan.

Meanwhile, put a large non-stick skillet over medium heat, add half the butter cubes, and heat until melted and frothy. Break the eggs gently into the pan, taking care not to burn your fingers or break the yolks. Season the whites lightly with a sprinkle of salt. Fry the eggs for 3–4 minutes until the yolks are just set, adding the remaining cubes of butter halfway.

Remove the eggs from the pan with a slotted spatula, drain, and place on the chargrilled side of the bottom piece of bread. Sprinkle with pepper and drizzle with ketchup. Top with the bread lid, chargrilled-side down, and cut in half. Eat right away.

KEY TO PERFECTION

When you're frying eggs, especially when there are several together in the same pan, it's tricky to get the yolks and whites cooked at the same time—the whites always set before the yolks. The trick is knowing how to speed up the cooking of the yolks.

As soon as the egg whites have set and the second addition of butter has melted, tilt the pan and spoon the hot butter over the egg yolks. Keep basting until an opaque white film sets over the yolks. This tells you that the yolks are done.

"If you sprinkle salt on the egg yolks before or during cooking, it will make them speckled and they won't cook evenly."

CLASSIC FRENCH OMELETTE

One of the first things you learn at catering college is how to cook an omelette, and a key question on the theory exam is: "What is the meaning of the word *baveuse*?" The answer is "cooked until moist in the center," which is the perfect description for a perfect omelette.

SERVES 1
3 extra large eggs, preferably organic
4 tbsp (½ stick) unsalted butter, diced
sea salt and freshly milled black pepper

Using a fork, lightly whisk the eggs in a bowl and season with salt and pepper.

Heat a 7in (17.5cm) non-stick skillet over medium-high heat. Add the butter and heat until foaming, then pour in the eggs. Shake the pan so the eggs run all over the bottom, then cook and stir with a spatula for 1–2 minutes so the butter gets mixed into the eggs, and the uncooked mixture runs to the sides of the pan.

When the eggs start to look softly set, season them lightly and remove the pan from the heat.

Fold two opposite edges to the center. Lift up one of the straight edges, then roll the omelette out of the pan onto a warmed plate. Press gently into a cigar shape with a clean cloth. Sprinkle with black pepper and serve immediately.

"If you're nervous about folding and rolling the omelette, just fold it in half to serve."

KEY TO PERFECTION

A classic French omelette should be the shape of a fat cigar, and it should ooze creaminess when you cut into it. To achieve this result, there are three key stages.

Whisk the eggs just until the yolks and whites are combined. Don't whisk too hard or you'll incorporate air, which will make an omelette tough.

Cook the eggs quickly and briefly—just until they are lightly set on the bottom but still runny on top. Don't be tempted to continue cooking or you'll lose the creamy consistency that is *baveuse*.

To get the characteristic shape of a classic French omelette, cover it with a cloth after rolling it onto the plate, then tuck the cloth in closely along the sides and press gently.

POACHED EGGS

A perfectly poached egg is a hallmark of a well-trained chef. When I was training at The Savoy in London, I'd watch the breakfast chef poach dozens of eggs every morning , and they were immaculate every time.

SERVES 2–4

4 extra large eggs, preferably organic

about ¹/₂ tsp white wine vinegar or malt vinegar

sea salt and freshly cracked black pepper

TO SERVE

4 English muffins

soft unsalted butter, for spreading

Get a bowl of water with ice cubes ready and set it aside. Fill a medium saucepan with water and bring to a boil. Meanwhile, crack one of the eggs into a small bowl or pitcher and add a drop of vinegar.

Whisk the boiling water to get it swirling, then slide the egg into the center. Turn the heat down to low and poach gently for 3 minutes. Remove the egg with a slotted spoon and lower it into the ice bath.

Poach the remaining eggs one at a time, scooping any scum from the surface of the water after each one. When the last egg is in the ice bath, wait for about 5 minutes for it to cool down, then lift out the eggs one at a time with the slotted spoon and trim around the whites with scissors. Drain the eggs on a cloth. (You can leave them like this, covered with plastic wrap, for up to 24 hours in the refrigerator.)

When ready to serve, bring a saucepan of water to a gentle simmer. Meanwhile, cut a thin slice off the tops of the muffins, toast on both sides, and spread with butter. Keep warm.

Gently reheat all 4 eggs together in the simmering water, allowing 2 minutes from the moment they are all in the pan. Lift them out, drain on a cloth or paper towels, and place on the muffins. Sprinkle with salt and pepper, and serve immediately.

ALL IS NOT LOST

If you overcook the eggs, chop them roughly and mix with finely chopped scallions, mayonnaise, Dijon mustard, and seasoning. This will make a perfect sandwich filling.

KEY TO PERFECTION

Both cooking and presentation are very important with poached eggs, as all too often they can be overcooked or look messy. The method in this recipe is a clever one, and easier than you think.

Whisk the boiling water vigorously, to create a whirlpool in the center. This will help keep the egg in shape when it first goes in.

Slip the egg into the whirlpool, then quickly lower the heat to a gentle simmer—don't let the water boil over or the egg will be spoiled.

As soon as the poached eggs are in the ice bath, they will stop cooking, and the yolks will stay runny.

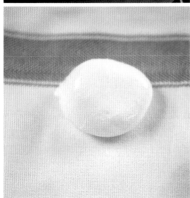

After trimming the whites to give a neat, professional edge, leave the eggs to drain on a kitchen towel.

OMELETTE ARNOLD BENNETT

This rich omelette has a fascinating history. The writer Arnold Bennett stayed at The Savoy hotel in 1929, to do research for his novel *The Imperial Palace*. While he was there, he asked the chef for a smoked haddock and cheese omelette so often that they named the dish after him. It was a flat omelette rather than a folded one, and it had become such a classic at the hotel over the years that it was one of the first things I put on the menu when I took over at the Savoy Grill.

SERVES 4
9oz (250g) undyed smoked
    haddock fillet, skinned
about 1¼ cups whole milk
8 extra large eggs, preferably
    organic
4 tbsp (½ stick) unsalted
    butter, diced
⅓ cup shredded sharp Cheddar
    or Gruyère cheese
4 tbsp heavy cream,
    lightly whipped

FOR THE HOLLANDAISE SAUCE
1 cup (2 sticks) unsalted
    butter, diced
7 tbsp white wine vinegar
juice of ½ lemon
3 extra large egg yolks,
    preferably organic
sea salt and cracked
    black pepper

First make the hollandaise sauce. Gently melt the butter in a small saucepan until the sediment sinks to the bottom. Pour the clear butter slowly into a glass measuring cup, leaving the sediment behind, and keep warm. Put the vinegar and lemon juice in another saucepan with a pinch each of salt and pepper. Boil until the liquid is reduced to about 3 tbsp. Strain through a fine sieve into a large bowl and let cool.

Mix the egg yolks into the vinegar reduction and set the bowl over a pan of simmering water (a *bain marie*). Whisk vigorously for about 5 minutes until thick and creamy white. Remove from the heat and gradually whisk in the melted butter, leaving behind any sediment in the bottom of the measuring cup. Set aside in a warm place.

Put the haddock in a pan with enough milk to cover. Poach gently for 5 minutes. Remove the fish with a slotted spoon and drain, then flake into large chunks, discarding any bones. Divide half of the chunks equally among four individual baking dishes. Keep warm.

Preheat the broiler.

Lightly whisk 4 of the eggs with salt and pepper. Heat a large, non-stick skillet over low heat until hot. Add half of the butter and, when hot, scramble the eggs (page 146) for about 2 minutes until soft and sloppy. Divide among the dishes, spooning the scrambled eggs over the fish, then dot the remaining fish on top.

Season and lightly whisk the remaining eggs. Heat the remaining butter and scramble the eggs as before, then spoon them over the fish and smooth the top with the back of a spoon. Cover each serving with one-fourth of the shredded cheese.

Fold the whipped cream into the hollandaise, dollop on top of each dish, and smooth over with the back of a spoon. Glaze the tops under the broiler and serve immediately.

KEY TO PERFECTION

For its signature smooth texture and buttery rich flavor, this unique dish hides a secret—hollandaise sauce. There are two key stages in the making of a perfect hollandaise.

The second stage is done off the heat, with the bowl removed from the *bain marie*. Very slowly pour the warm (not hot) melted butter into the egg mix, whisking the whole time so the butter is smoothly incorporated without separating. When the last of the butter has gone in, you should have a thick and creamy emulsion.

For the first stage, the egg yolks and vinegar reduction must be whisked to the right consistency. To check, lift the whisk out of the mixture and move it across the surface—it should leave a ribbon trail behind it.

ALL IS NOT LOST

If the sauce curdles, drop in a few ice cubes and whisk vigorously until the sauce is smooth again.

PANCAKES

Homemade pancakes are infinitely better than any that you buy frozen or prepare from a mix. I just love cooking these while everyone sits around the table waiting for them to come out of the pan. My eldest son Jake and I both like our pancakes topped with thick slices of butter and doused in plenty of maple syrup.

MAKES ABOUT 36
1²/₃ cups all-purpose flour
2¹/₂ tsp baking powder
¹/₂ tsp fine table salt
¹/₂ tsp ground cinnamon
¹/₄ cup granulated sugar
4 extra large eggs, preferably organic, separated
2 cups milk
6 tbsp (³/₄ stick) unsalted butter, melted and cooled
1 tsp almond extract
2 extra large egg whites, preferably organic
vegetable oil, for frying

TO SERVE
confectioners' sugar
unsalted butter
maple syrup

Sift the flour into a large bowl with the baking powder, salt, and cinnamon. Stir in the granulated sugar, reserving 1 tbsp for later.

Whisk the 4 egg yolks in a medium bowl until thickened, then gradually whisk in the milk, melted butter, and almond extract.

Make a well in the dry ingredients. Slowly pour in the egg yolk mixture, whisking constantly to make a smooth batter.

Put the 6 egg whites in a clean bowl and whisk to soft peaks, adding the reserved sugar halfway through. Fold into the batter.

Set a large, non-stick skillet over medium heat. Splash in a little oil to cover the bottom of the pan and heat until hot. Spoon the batter into the pan to make four pancakes, each 3¹/₂–4in (8–10cm) in diameter. Cook for 2–2¹/₂ minutes until the underside is golden brown, then turn the pancakes over and cook for 1¹/₂–2 minutes longer to lightly brown the other side.

Lift the pancakes out of the pan with a spatula and serve immediately, with confectioners' sugar, butter, and syrup.

Make more pancakes in the same way, cooking them four at a time and adding more oil when necessary. They are best served straight from the pan, or as soon as possible after cooking.

KEY TO PERFECTION

The secret of great pancakes is aeration—getting air into the batter at the beginning and keeping it there while the pancakes are cooking.

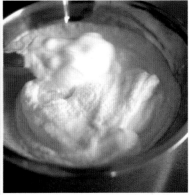

Mix a spoonful of the egg whites into the batter to loosen it slightly, then tip the rest on top of the batter and gently fold them in with a rubber spatula until evenly incorporated. Work gently and slowly to retain the air. Don't tap, whisk, or bang the bowl while you're folding or you'll knock out the air.

First, whisk the egg whites to soft, snowy peaks that are full of air. Using a balloon whisk, this should only take a minute or two—just until the peaks flop over when you stop beating.

"A bouncy, bendy balloon whisk is best for incorporating air, and it makes the job easy. Don't use a stiff, inflexible whisk or you'll have to work twice as hard."

ALL IS NOT LOST

If you leave the whisked egg whites to stand before folding them into the batter, they will curdle and become watery underneath. Don't worry. Just throw in a small handful of sugar to stabilize the mixture, and whisk until soft peaks form again.

CRÊPES

One of the secrets behind making crêpes successfully is to use the right pan. This used to be a steel pan, which you had to keep well seasoned, but nowadays non-stick skillets are the best and easiest. I like crêpes served simply, with just a sprinkle of sugar and a squeeze of lemon.

MAKES 6
1 extra large egg, preferably
   organic
²/₃ cup self-rising flour
pinch of fine table salt
1¹/₄ cups whole milk
vegetable oil, for frying

TO SERVE
granulated sugar
lemon wedges

Lightly whisk the egg in a bowl, add the flour and salt, and slowly whisk in the milk. Whisk out the lumps, then strain the batter into a bowl or large measuring cup. Refrigerate for about 30 minutes.

Put an 8in (20cm) non-stick skillet over medium-high heat, swirl a thin film of oil over the bottom of the pan, and heat until you can see a light haze rising.

Pour off the excess oil, then ladle in enough batter to coat the bottom of the pan in a thin layer. Put the pan back on the heat and cook the crêpe for 2–3 minutes until the underside is colored.

Flip the crêpe over and cook the other side for 1–2 minutes, then slide the crêpe out of the pan. Serve immediately, either rolled or folded, with sugar and lemon wedges. Continue making crêpes until all the batter is used, adding more oil when necessary.

KEY TO PERFECTION

Crêpes should be lacy thin, so you must have lump-free batter and only use a very small amount at a time. Slow but sure is the way to work.

After whisking the batter with a balloon whisk until it's as smooth as you can get it, pour it through a sieve to catch any minute lumps of flour that remain.

To cook a crêpe, tilt the pan toward you, then swish in a ladleful of batter and tilt and roll the pan from side to side. The batter should flow right to the edge. If it doesn't quite cover, fill any gaps by ladling in a little more batter.

To see if the crêpe is ready to flip over, lift up a corner and check that it is set and light golden underneath. If it is, shake the pan to release the bottom of the crêpe, and flip it over to cook the second side.

DESSERTS

VANILLA PANNA COTTA

Panna cotta means "cooked cream" in Italian, and it is one of the easiest desserts to make. To appreciate its texture fully, use the best heavy cream you can find. Most health food stores carry pasteurized (not ultrapasteurized) cream, which has the perfect rich flavor.

SERVES 4
1 1/2 leaves gelatin
1 cup plus 6 tbsp heavy cream
1/4 cup whole milk
1/2 cup granulated sugar
1 1/2 vanilla beans
1 tbsp dark rum or orange
   liqueur

Soak the gelatin leaves in ice water for about 10 minutes until they are soft.

Meanwhile, put the cream, milk, and sugar in a heavy pan. Split the vanilla beans lengthwise and scrape the seeds out into the pan, then drop in the pods. Bring to a boil, stirring occasionally. Add the rum and stir to mix. Take the pan off the heat.

Remove the gelatin leaves from the water and squeeze firmly. Add to the hot cream mixture and whisk until completely dissolved.

Strain the mix through a fine sieve into a large liquid measuring cup and discard the vanilla beans. Stand the measuring cup in a bowl of ice water. Stir frequently until the mixture starts to thicken, then pour into four 3in (8cm) diameter ramekins or custard cups. Refrigerate for 1–2 hours until set.

To serve, run the tip of a small, sharp knife around the top edge of each panna cotta to release it from the side of the ramekin. Dip the bottom of each ramekin in hot water for a few seconds, then turn the panna cotta out onto a plate.

"If you don't stir the panna cotta mix enough while it's thickening, it can set on the inside of the measuring cup. If this happens, warm it gently by standing the cup in a pan of warm water, then cool it down again in the ice bath, stirring all the time."

KEY TO PERFECTION

Gelatin leaves give a smoother set than powder, and they're easier to use, too. You can find them at specialty baking stores and online. If you want to use powdered gelatin, substitute 1 envelope for 4 leaves and follow the package directions for dissolving.

Immerse the brittle leaves in a bowl of cold water to which you've added a few ice cubes. After about 10 minutes, the leaves will soften and become pliable.

Take the softened leaves out of the water and squeeze them tightly to get rid of as much surplus water as possible.

Drop the gelatin into the hot cream mixture while whisking constantly, or the gelatin will sink to the bottom in a clump. Keep whisking until the gelatin has completely dissolved.

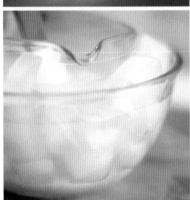
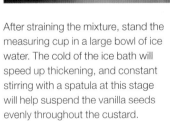

After straining the mixture, stand the measuring cup in a large bowl of ice water. The cold of the ice bath will speed up thickening, and constant stirring with a spatula at this stage will help suspend the vanilla seeds evenly throughout the custard.

STRAWBERRY FOOL

This is one of the best ways to use overripe fruit that has plenty of flavor. The fruit is cooked into a purée, then folded into whipped cream and yogurt to make a soft, spoonable dessert. Other berries can be used, too. Just adjust the sugar to taste.

SERVES 6
2¼lb (1kg) soft, ripe
  strawberries, hulled and
  quartered lengthwise
juice of ½ lemon
⅓ cup plus 1 tbsp granulated
  sugar
2 leaves gelatin
1 cup heavy cream
1 cup thick, plain yogurt,
  preferably Greek

TO FINISH
⅔ cup heavy cream
1 tbsp sifted confectioners'
  sugar

Place a large, heavy saucepan over medium to high heat. When hot, put in the strawberries, lemon juice, and granulated sugar. Cook for about 15 minutes, stirring frequently. Remove from the heat.

Soak the gelatin leaves in ice water for about 10 minutes until soft. Meanwhile, pour the contents of the saucepan into a blender and purée until smooth. Transfer to a large bowl.

Remove the gelatin from the water and squeeze dry, then stir into the warm purée until dissolved. Cover and refrigerate for about half an hour until chilled but not set. Lightly whip 1 cup cream.

Stir the yogurt into the purée, then fold in the whipped cream until evenly mixed. Divide equally among six glasses. Cover and refrigerate for at least 6 hours, preferably overnight.

To finish, lightly whip the remaining cream with the confectioners' sugar until it just holds its shape. Spoon on top of the fools. Serve immediately or keep in the refrigerator for up to 2 hours before serving.

KEY TO PERFECTION

Most recipes for fruit fools have a raw purée as their base, but cooked fruit gives a smoother finish. This is simplicity itself to achieve, but often overlooked.

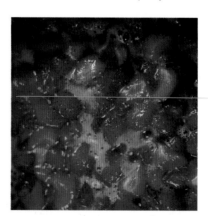

Cook the strawberries with the sugar and lemon juice until reduced down slightly, and you can see that all the pieces of fruit are very soft. Stir frequently to make sure they all cook evenly.

"Only make this fool with locally grown strawberries in season, when they're ripe and bursting with flavor. If strawberries are hard and tasteless when they're raw, they won't be any better cooked."

LEMON POSSET WITH WARM SPICED FRUITS

Posset is a creamy dessert that has its roots in English medieval cookery, so it seems right to partner it with spiced mixed fruits that evoke the scent and flavor of mulled wine. The extreme temperature contrast of warm fruits and chilled posset works really well.

SERVES 6
about 5 large lemons
3²/₃ cups heavy cream
1¹/₄ cups granulated sugar

FOR THE SPICED FRUITS
3 stems of rhubarb, leaves and
    root ends trimmed
3 red plums
a small handful of blueberries
    or black currants (optional)
a handful each of blackberries
    and raspberries
4 tbsp (¹/₄ stick) unsalted
    butter, diced
³/₄ cup granulated sugar
2 cinnamon sticks
6 star anise
2 vanilla beans, split lengthwise
3–4 tbsp dark rum (optional)

Finely grate the zest from the lemons. Halve the lemons and squeeze out the juice, then strain and measure it—you need 1 cup.

Mix the cream, lemon zest, and sugar in a non-stick saucepan. Bring to a boil, stirring occasionally until the sugar has dissolved, then simmer for 3 minutes. Take the pan off the heat and whisk in the lemon juice. Strain the mix into a glass measuring cup, pressing the zest in the sieve to extract as much flavor as possible. Discard the zest.

Skim the froth off the top of the posset mix, then pour equal amounts into six dessert glasses, leaving about 1in (2.5cm) at the top to make room for the fruit topping. Leave to cool. Cover the glasses with plastic wrap and refrigerate for at least 24 hours.

When you are ready to serve, prepare and cook the fruits. Cut the rhubarb into ¹/₂in (1cm) lozenges. Halve and pit the plums, then cut the halves lengthwise down the middle and cut each quarter into four equal pieces. If using black currants, trim the ends.

Heat a heavy saucepan over medium heat. Add the diced butter and heat until foaming, then add the rhubarb and plums. Sauté the fruits for about 5 minutes until they start to soften, then add the blueberries or currants (if using), the sugar, cinnamon sticks, and star anise. Scrape the seeds out of the vanilla beans into the pan and drop in the pods, too. Stir the fruit well and add the rum (if using), then cook for 5–8 minutes longer. Take the pan off the heat, remove the whole spices and vanilla beans, and fold in the blackberries and raspberries.

Serve the possets chilled, topped with the hot spiced fruits.

KEY TO PERFECTION

The addition of a precise amount of lemon juice is crucial to the success of a posset. The acid starts off a chemical reaction in the cream, and this makes it set when it's chilled in the refrigerator.

An old-fashioned reamer is one of the best tools for getting the maximum juice out of a lemon. Use it over a sieve to catch all the seeds and pith, then pour the strained juice into a measuring cup.

EARL GREY TEA CREAM

With its subtle, citrus-like perfume, Earl Grey is the perfect tea to flavor this delicate, smooth, creamy dessert. Made in tea cups, the end result looks exactly like a cup of tea with milk.

SERVES 6
1 cup plus 2 tbsp whole milk
1 cup plus 2 tbsp heavy cream
7 Earl Grey teabags
2/3 cup granulated sugar
5–6 extra large egg yolks,
   preferably organic

TO SERVE
1/2 vanilla bean, cut lengthwise
   into 6 very thin sticks
Butter Shortbread (page 202),
   cut into fingers

Preheat the oven to 300°F (150°C).

Put the milk, cream, and teabags in a heavy saucepan with half of the sugar. Bring to a boil over medium to high heat, stirring occasionally, then immediately strain through a fine sieve into a bowl, squeezing the teabags gently in the sieve.

Whisk the egg yolks in a large bowl with the remaining sugar until well combined. Pour in the tea milk and whisk well. Strain slowly through a fine sieve into another bowl, then skim to remove any foamy bubbles.

Stand six ovenproof teacups or ramekins (3/4 cup capacity) in a roasting pan. Slowly pour the tea cream into the cups to fill them two-thirds full, then skim off any more bubbles. Add hot water to the roasting pan. Bake in the middle of the oven for 25–30 minutes. The tea creams are ready when their centers have a slight, but firm quiver when you shake the pan very gently. Remove the cups from the water and let cool.

Refrigerate the tea creams for at least 4 hours, or overnight. Serve chilled, with a vanilla stick popped into each one, and shortbread fingers.

KEY TO PERFECTION

Tea creams depend on very gentle cooking for their delicate, silky smoothness. The oven temperature is low, but you should also remove all air bubbles from the cream mixture before cooking, and then bake in a hot water bath called a *bain marie*.

Carefully skim the surface of the strained mixture using a spoon. Even one bubble can spoil the appearance of the finished cream.

Pour hot water into the roasting pan to come halfway up the sides of the cups. This *bain marie* will protect the tea creams from the heat of the oven, preventing them from getting too hot.

"Don't leave the teabags to stand or steep in the milk, or the tea cream will taste stewed and bitter."

CUSTARD TART

The original recipe for this tart was my grandmother's, and I made it for Queen Elizabeth's 80th birthday lunch in London. I think it's as close to perfection as any custard tart can be.

SERVES 6–8
1 quantity chilled Sweet
  Shortcrust Pastry (below)
2 large egg yolks, preferably
  organic, lightly beaten,
  to glaze

FOR THE FILLING
9 large egg yolks, preferably
  organic
1/3 cup plus 1 tbsp granulated
  sugar
2 cups heavy cream
1 whole nutmeg, for grating

Place a buttered 9in (23cm) tart pan with a removable bottom on a baking sheet lined with parchment paper. Roll out the pastry dough and chill it for half an hour, then use to line the tart pan, letting the surplus dough hang over the top. Chill the pastry shell for half an hour.

Preheat the oven to 375°F (190°C).

Blind-bake the pastry shell for 10 minutes until it starts to turn golden brown. Remove the paper and rice, and brush inside the pastry shell with the egg yolks. Return to the oven to bake for 5 minutes longer. Leave to cool. Turn the oven down to 300°F (150°C).

Next make the filling. Put the egg yolks and sugar in a bowl and whisk to combine. Add the cream and mix well, then strain the mixture through a fine sieve into a heavy saucepan. Warm over low heat until just tepid (about 98°F/37°C), stirring all the time. Pour into a pitcher.

Put the cooled pastry shell, still in its pan on the baking sheet, on the middle shelf of the oven. Slowly and carefully pour in the custard, filling the shell as full as you can—right to the very top. Grate nutmeg liberally all over, to cover the custard completely.

Bake the tart for about 45 minutes until the custard looks set but not too firm—it should have a slight, even quiver across the top when you gently shake the baking sheet. Leave to cool to room temperature, then remove from the pan. Cut into wedges with a sharp knife to serve.

SWEET SHORTCRUST PASTRY

1 1/2 cups all-purpose flour, sifted
  with a pinch of fine table salt
10 tbsp (1 1/4 sticks) chilled
  unsalted butter, diced
1/3 cup plus 1 tbsp granulated
  sugar
finely grated zest of 1 lemon
1 large egg, preferably
  organic, beaten

In a large bowl, gently work the flour and butter together until the mix looks like bread crumbs. Stir in the sugar and lemon zest, then add the eggs slowly to form a dough. Gently shape it into a ball and flatten slightly, then wrap tightly in plastic wrap and refrigerate for 2 hours before using. This pastry dough is very fragile, and handles best when it is well chilled but not hard.

KEY TO PERFECTION

Crisp, melt-in-the-mouth pastry is the hallmark of this traditional English tart. The trick is to get both the pastry dough and the pastry shell right. If there are any holes or cracks, the filling will ooze out during baking and make the pastry wet.

Start making the dough by adding the butter in small pieces to the flour and salt, picking up the butter and flour mixture and letting it roll through your fingers. Repeat, gently rubbing with your fingers, until all the butter is incorporated with the flour and the mix looks like bread crumbs.

Mix in the sugar, lemon zest, and eggs with one hand, stroking the mixture and turning the bowl at the same time. As soon as the dough comes together, turn it out onto a well-floured surface. Shape it gently into a ball, then pat lightly to flatten. Don't overwork it.

With a well-floured rolling pin, roll out the dough on a well-floured surface until 1/8in (3mm) thick. Don't stretch the dough while rolling, but keep turning it around and patting in the edges with floured hands until you have a disk about 3in (8cm) larger than the tart pan. Place the disk between two sheets of floured waxed paper and chill for half an hour.

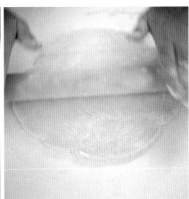

Roll some dough trimmings into a ball and dust with flour, then press the ball into the bottom inside edge of the pastry shell and up the side to make them smooth. If there are any cracks, press them together with your fingers. Chill again for half an hour.

Trim the edge of the disk to make it neat, then lift it on the rolling pin and drop into the pan. Ease in gently with floured hands, letting the dough hang over the top and down the outside of the pan.

Set the shape of the pastry shell by baking it without the filling (blind-baking): line it with parchment paper, fill with uncooked rice, and put it in the oven to bake.

After 10 minutes, remove the paper and rice, then brush all over the inside of the pastry shell with beaten egg yolk. Bake for 5 minutes longer. This will seal the pastry so the filling can't seep into it and make it soggy.

When the pastry shell is cool enough to handle, it's ready to be filled. It will be crisp and golden, both inside and out.

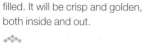

To release the tart from the pan before serving, work around the top edge with a serrated knife using a sawing action—the excess pastry will drop away and then you can lift off the outside ring of the pan.

ALL IS NOT LOST

If cracks appear in the pastry shell during blind-baking, don't leave them or the filling will ooze out. Patch up the cracks with scraps of raw pastry dough and bake for an additional 5 minutes.

TREACLE TART

Golden syrup, similar to corn syrup but made from cane sugar, is a staple ingredient in British kitchens, and the traditional sweetener for this tart filling (you can buy golden syrup at many U.S. supermarkets and online). The filling has a wonderful moist, cakey texture and rich, toasty flavor that is unusual but addictive.

SERVES 10–12

1 quantity chilled Sweet
   Shortcrust Pastry (page 172)
2 large egg yolks, preferably
   organic, lightly beaten,
   to glaze

FOR THE FILLING

1¹/₄ cups golden syrup
¹/₂ cup plus 1 tbsp almond
   flour or finely ground
   blanched almonds
2 cups fresh bread crumbs
   (make in a blender)
2 large eggs, preferably
   organic, beaten
²/₃ cup heavy cream

Mix all the filling ingredients in a large bowl until well combined. Cover and refrigerate overnight.

Put a buttered 10in (25cm) tart pan with a removable bottom on a baking sheet lined with parchment paper. Roll out the pastry dough on a well-floured surface to a disk about 3in (8cm) larger than the tart pan, then chill between two sheets of floured waxed paper for half an hour.

Line the pan with the pastry (page 173), pressing it smoothly into the bottom inside edge and up the side, and letting it hang over the top and down the outside of the pan. Chill for another half an hour.

Preheat the oven to 375°F (190°C).

Blind-bake the pastry shell for 10 minutes (page 174) until it starts to turn golden brown. Remove the paper and rice, brush the inside of the pastry case with the egg yolks, and return to the oven to bake for 5 minutes. Leave to cool. Keep the oven at the same temperature.

Stir the filling, then pour it into the cooled pastry shell. Leave to settle for a few minutes, then place the tart in the middle of the oven and bake for 10 minutes.

Turn the oven down to 325°F (170°C) and bake the tart for about 35 minutes longer until the filling is a deep caramel brown, and firm when gently touched in the middle.

Leave the tart to settle for 10–15 minutes, then saw off the overhanging pastry using a serrated knife. Carefully lift off the side of the pan. Serve the tart warm or cold.

KEY TO PERFECTION

The filling must be made the day before baking to allow time for the bread crumbs to absorb the golden syrup and swell, and the pastry shell must be partially baked before the filling goes in. These are the secrets of a deep-filled and moist treacle tart with crisp, sweet pastry.

When you stir the filling ingredients together at the outset, the mixture will be thin and runny.

After refrigerating overnight, stir the filling again. It will be very thick.

Pour the thickened filling into the partially baked pastry shell, then place in the oven to bake until richly colored.

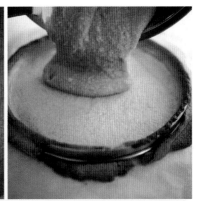

DEEP-DISH APPLE PIE

I always make apple pie this way, with two different types of apples. Those for the base break down into a firm applesauce, while the crisp apples for the top retain their shape so slices look pretty when the pie is cut. With its crisp, buttery pastry, it's sheer perfection.

SERVES 8–10

1 quantity chilled Sweet
   Shortcrust Pastry (page 172)
1/2 cup granulated sugar mixed
   with 1 tsp ground cinnamon
1 large egg white, preferably
   organic, lightly beaten

FOR THE FILLING

6 large McIntosh or Rome
   apples, about 31/4lb
   (1.5kg) total weight
2 tbsp unsalted butter, diced
2–3 cinnamon sticks, broken
   into large pieces
3/4 cup granulated sugar
5 medium Golden Delicious or
   Granny Smith apples

Peel, quarter, and core the McIntosh apples, then chop into small pieces. Warm a large, heavy saucepan over medium heat. Add the butter and wait until it starts to foam, then add the cinnamon sticks and sauté for 2–3 minutes to get the spicy aroma going. Add the apple pieces and the sugar, and cook uncovered for about 20 minutes until fairly dry, stirring occasionally. Pour the applesauce out of the pan and spread over a large plate. Leave until cold.

Meanwhile, roll out two-thirds of the pastry dough on a well-floured surface to 1/4in (5mm) thick. Use to line a loose-bottomed 8 x 2in (20 x 5cm) springform pan, patching any cracks and letting the dough hang over the top. Set the springform pan on a baking sheet. Roll out the remaining pastry dough to make a lid 1/8in (3mm) thick and place between two sheets of floured waxed paper. Refrigerate the pastry shell and lid for 1 hour.

Spread the cold applesauce in the chilled pastry shell, discarding the cinnamon. Peel the Golden Delicious apples, halve them lengthwise, and cut out the cores. Slice the apples 1/8in (3mm) thick. Arrange the apple slices overlapping on top of the applesauce, spiraling them in from the edge and doming in the center. Sprinkle them with some of the cinnamon sugar as you layer them.

Brush the edge of the pastry shell with egg white. Place the chilled pastry lid carefully on top and press the edges together. Trim off excess dough, then seal the edges together by pressing with a fork. Cut two or three slits in the center of the lid. Refrigerate for 1 hour.

Preheat the oven to 400°F (200°C).

Lightly brush the pie lid with egg white and sprinkle with some of the remaining cinnamon sugar, then bake on the baking sheet for 55–60 minutes, covering the top with foil if it becomes too brown. Leave the pie to cool for about half an hour before removing it from the pan. Sprinkle with more cinnamon sugar before serving.

KEY TO PERFECTION

The applesauce needs to be quite dry. If it is wet, it will seep into the pastry shell and make the pie soggy.

Start cooking the McIntosh apple pieces over medium heat with the butter, cinnamon, and sugar—they will soon break down to a pulp.

Just before the end of the cooking time, increase the heat to high and stir vigorously—this will drive off the moisture and help the applesauce become thick and dry.

"To turn this pie into a tart, make the pastry shell slightly thicker and leave the lid off. The tart will cook in about two-thirds of the time."

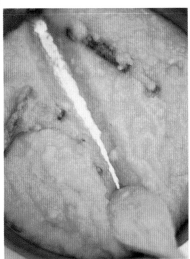

NEW YORK CHEESECAKE

This is the real thing—a rich, creamy, baked cheesecake. It's perfect plain, but to cut through the richness I sometimes serve it with a blueberry compote sharpened with a bit of lemon juice. Long, slow baking gives the cheesecake the smoothest texture imaginable.

SERVES 8–10

- 3 tbsp unsalted butter, melted and cooled
- 1 cup graham cracker crumbs
- 1lb 2oz (500g) cream cheese, at room temperature
- 1 cup granulated sugar
- 1/3 cup heavy cream
- 3 tbsp cornstarch
- 4 large eggs, preferably organic, beaten

Preheat the oven to 225°F (120°C). Put a 9 x 3in (23 x 8cm) springform pan on a baking sheet.

Mix the melted butter with the graham cracker crumbs. Press over the bottom of the pan to make a smooth, even layer that goes tight into the corners.

Put the cream cheese in a bowl and mix in the sugar, cream, and cornstarch using a rubber spatula. Pour in the eggs and beat together until really smooth.

Pour the mix over the cracker crust. Shake the pan to level the filling and smooth the top.

Bake the cheesecake on the middle shelf of the oven for 1 1/2 hours until just set but still with a little wobble in the center. Let cool to room temperature before removing the sides of the pan.

KEY TO PERFECTION

Baked cheesecakes are richer and more satisfying than cheesecakes set with gelatin, which tend to be light and fluffy. To get the dreamy, creamy texture that makes a baked cheesecake so special, you need to pay attention to detail before baking.

The cream cheese filling must be well mixed so there are no lumps. It will then pour evenly over the cracker crust, which must be flat.

Once the filling is level in the pan, smooth over the top with your fingertip to remove any air bubbles. This will prevent uneven rising, so the top of the cheesecake will bake perfectly flat.

"Always use a full-fat cream cheese for this classic cheesecake—low-fat cheese won't give the right creamy texture—and don't refrigerate the cheesecake or it will go rock solid."

CREAMY RICE PUDDING

There are many ways to make rice pudding. I prefer a pudding to be stirred on top of the stove rather than baked. This is my extra-rich version. Starchy short-grain rice is essential as it contributes to the pudding's creamy texture.

SERVES 4
scant ½ cup short-grain rice,
   such as Arborio, Baldo,
   or Japanese sushi rice
1 cup whole milk
1 cup heavy cream
1 vanilla bean, split lengthwise,
   and seeds scraped out
   and reserved
5 extra large egg yolks,
   preferably organic
½ cup granulated sugar
jam, to serve

Rinse and drain the rice, then pour into a heavy saucepan. Add the milk and cream and drop in the vanilla bean (not the seeds). Bring to a boil over medium heat, stirring occasionally. Turn the heat down to low and simmer gently, stirring from time to time, for about 20 minutes until the rice is soft but still with a slight bite.

Put the egg yolks in a bowl with the sugar and vanilla seeds, and whisk to combine.

Take the pan of rice from the heat and remove the vanilla bean. Mix about one-third of the rice with the egg yolks, then stir this mix into the rest of the rice in the pan. Continue cooking over low heat for a few more minutes, stirring constantly, until the pudding is thick enough to coat the back of the spoon.

Pour the pudding into bowls and put a spoonful of jam in the center of each. If you like, give the rice a baked look by flashing a propane torch briefly over the top. Serve hot.

"This rice pudding is so rich and creamy that it's just as good cold as hot. For a change from jam, try serving it with warmed, sliced apricots or peaches topped with a sprinkling of cinnamon and toasted sliced almonds."

KEY TO PERFECTION

Egg yolks make this rice pudding wonderfully thick, rich, and creamy, but you must prevent them from overheating or they might curdle.

Don't add the egg yolk mixture to the hot rice all at once. Instead, take the pan off the heat and make a *liaison* by slowly whisking one-third of the hot rice into the egg yolk mixture a spoonful at a time. This is called tempering, and it helps prevent the yolks from curdling.

With the pan back on the heat, stir the egg yolk *liaison* into the rice pudding in the pan. Use a wooden spatula and stir continuously so the pudding does not stick to the bottom. Stirring also keeps the mixture on the move, which helps prevent the liquid from overheating and curdling.

When you can draw a finger smoothly through the pudding coating the back of the spatula, you know the egg yolks have done their job.

ALL IS NOT LOST

If you've let the pudding get too hot and you can see it starting to separate, whip the pan off the heat and quickly beat in a splash of cold cream. This will cool the pudding down and stop it from curdling.

TREACLE SPONGE PUDDING

From the tradition of British steamed desserts comes this warm, very moist, cake-like treat. It is lighter than most, with a nice citrus flavor from the orange juice and zest to balance the sweet syrup. Try it with whipped cream or vanilla ice cream.

SERVES 4–6

1 cup golden syrup, plus extra warmed syrup to serve

finely grated zest and juice of 2 oranges

12 tbsp (1¾ sticks) softened unsalted butter, plus extra for the bowl

¾ cup plus 1 tbsp packed light brown sugar

3 extra large eggs, preferably organic, beaten

1 tsp unsulfured molasses

1 cup plus 3 tbsp self-rising flour, sifted

Brush a 1-quart (1-liter) ceramic bowl with butter. Mix the golden syrup with the orange zest and juice, and pour into the bottom of the bowl. Set aside.

Beat the butter and sugar together until light and fluffy, using an electric mixer or a wooden spoon. Slowly add the eggs, beating well. Add the molasses, then fold in the flour until evenly mixed.

Spoon the batter into the bowl and smooth the top. Don't worry when the syrup oozes up the side—this will make the pudding moist. Cover tightly and steam in a covered pan half filled with boiling water for 2 hours, checking the water level regularly to prevent boiling dry.

Uncover the pudding and unmold it onto a plate. Pour warmed golden syrup over the top and serve immediately.

KEY TO PERFECTION

It's essential to cover the bowl properly before steaming, both to allow room for the pudding to rise, and to prevent water and steam from getting into the mixture and making it unpleasantly soggy.

Make a parchment paper *cartouche* (page 88) that is 2in (5cm) larger than the top of the bowl. Lay the *cartouche* over the top of the bowl and fold a deep pleat in the center.

Fold the *cartouche* down over the edge of the bowl and tie it securely under the rim with string.

Lay a large sheet of foil over the *cartouche*, then crumple and fold it under the rim to seal.

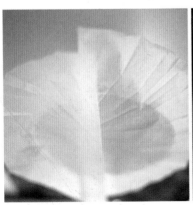

CRISP TOPPING WITH CUSTARD

To prevent the topping for a fruit crisp from getting soggy from the fruit underneath, it's best to cook the fruit and topping separately. To be honest, I like the crisp topping so much that I often skip the fruit altogether, and serve it with a hot custard sauce.

SERVES 6

12 tbsp (1½ sticks) unsalted butter, slightly softened

¾ cup plus 1 tbsp demerara sugar or packed light brown sugar

1¾ cups plus 2 tbsp all-purpose flour, sifted

1¼ cups toasted and chopped hazelnuts

FOR THE CUSTARD SAUCE

6 extra large egg yolks, preferably organic

⅓ cup granulated sugar

2 tsp custard powder or cornstarch

1 cup whole milk

1 cup heavy cream

1 vanilla bean, split in half lengthwise

Preheat the oven to 400°F (200°C).

Rub the butter, sugar, and flour together in a bowl with your fingertips until the mix looks like coarse bread crumbs. Stir in the hazelnuts. Press the mixture evenly over a large baking pan (about 9 x 13in/23 x 33cm). Bake for 30–35 minutes until crisp and golden.

Meanwhile, make the custard sauce. Whisk the egg yolks, sugar, and custard powder in a large bowl, then set aside. Pour the milk and cream into a heavy saucepan. Scrape the seeds from the vanilla bean halves into the pan and drop in the pod, too. Bring to a boil.

Slowly whisk the hot milk and cream into the yolk mixture, then pour back into the pan and bring to a boil, stirring with a spatula. Cook over low to medium heat for about 5 minutes until thickened, stirring constantly with the spatula and scraping it around the bottom and edge of the pan.

Break the topping into rough pieces and divide among six bowls. Strain the hot custard, pour it over the topping, and serve.

KEY TO PERFECTION

Using custard powder stabilizes the egg yolks so the custard can be heated to a boil without curdling. This makes a soothing, steaming hot custard with no floury taste.

Whisk the egg yolks and sugar together first, then sprinkle the custard powder over the top. If the powder goes in too soon, it will be difficult to get rid of any lumps.

Continue whisking vigorously until smooth. If not used immediately, whisk the mixture again before adding the hot milk and cream.

CHOCOLATE FONDANT CAKES

Thanks to the world-wide influence of the globe-trotting chef, Jean-Georges Vongerichten, this wickedly rich, warm dessert is a favorite on both sides of the Atlantic. Be sure to use the very best chocolate you can find.

SERVES 6

2 large eggs, preferably organic, at room temperature

2 large egg yolks, preferably organic, at room temperature

²/₃ cup granulated sugar

3oz (90g) high-quality bittersweet chocolate (at least 70% cocoa solids), finely chopped

6 tbsp (¹/₂ stick plus 2 tbsp) softened unsalted butter, plus extra for the rings

¹/₃ cup all-purpose flour, sifted

Butter the inside of six metal rings that are 2in (5cm) in diameter and 2in (5cm) tall. Line each ring with parchment paper to come just above the top. Stand them on a parchment-lined baking sheet.

Whisk the whole eggs in a bowl, add the egg yolks and sugar, and whisk again until evenly combined.

Melt the chocolate and butter very gently in a bowl set over a pan of hot water (a *bain marie*) or a double boiler. Remove the bowl from the pan and stir the chocolate gently. Cool for a minute or two, then whisk the chocolate into the egg mixture. Add the flour and whisk well to ensure there are no lumps. Chill for 30 minutes.

Spoon the mixture into the parchment-lined rings, filling them about two-thirds full. Refrigerate for 3–4 hours until set.

Preheat the oven to 400°F (200°C).

Bake the cakes in the middle of the oven for 10 minutes. Remove from the oven and let rest for 2 minutes, then very carefully lift the metal rings up and off, and gently peel off the paper. With a spatula, transfer the cakes to small plates, taking care not to puncture them as they are soft. Serve immediately.

"If you don't have small metal rings, you can make and serve these cakes in small ramekins."

KEY TO PERFECTION

For these cakes to have their signature gooey centers, you must handle the chocolate with gentle care. If it becomes too hot during melting, or if water gets into it, the chocolate can become grainy or "seize" into a hard lump.

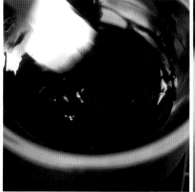

Both the egg mixture and the melted chocolate must be at the same temperature when they are whisked together. If the eggs are cold, straight from the refrigerator, they will make the chocolate "split" and look grainy.

Melt the chocolate and butter in a *bain marie*. Make sure the heat under the pan is low, and that the base of the bowl is not touching the water. A bowl with a lip that fits snugly over the pan is best, to prevent moisture from seeping up the sides into the chocolate.

ALL IS NOT LOST

If the chocolate sets in a hard ball or becomes grainy, you can't use it for the cakes, but you can easily turn it into truffles. Stir in 1/2 cup heavy cream, then pour into a deep tray and chill until set. Roll into balls, or scoop with a melon baller dipped in hot water, and roll in cocoa powder. Chill until firm, then roll in more cocoa powder.

CHOCOLATE-DIPPED MERINGUES

One New Year's Eve, something went wrong in the pastry section of the kitchen at Pétrus, in London. Luckily my head chef, Darren, was able to make these at the drop of a hat. They can be served as a dessert or as a petit four, and they're great for parties.

MAKES ABOUT 25
a wedge of lemon
3 extra large egg whites,
    preferably organic
1 cup superfine sugar

FOR THE FILLING
7oz (200g) high-quality
    bittersweet chocolate
    (at least 70% cocoa solids),
    finely chopped
1 cup heavy cream
3 tbsp confectioners' sugar,
    sifted

Preheat the oven to 225°F (120°C). Line two large baking sheets with parchment paper.

Rub a lemon wedge over the inside of your electric mixer bowl. Put the egg whites in the bowl and beat to soft peaks on low to medium speed. Increase the speed to high and continue beating, adding the sugar gradually until the meringue is stiff.

Pipe twenty-five 2in (5cm) rosettes of meringue on each parchment-lined baking sheet, using a pastry bag fitted with a 1/2in (1cm) star tip. Bake for about 1 hour until firm and crisp, swapping the baking sheets around halfway through baking. Lift the meringues, still on their parchment sheets, off the baking sheets and leave to cool. Line the baking sheets with clean parchment paper.

Meanwhile, make the filling. Melt the chocolate in a *bain marie* (pages 190–191), then remove from the heat. Dip the flat base of each meringue in the chocolate, then place them chocolate-side down on the clean parchment paper. Refrigerate until set.

Whip the cream with the confectioners' sugar until firm. Use to put the meringues together in pairs, chocolate sides into the center. Serve immediately or keep in the refrigerator for up to 2 hours.

"If you can spare the time, let the meringues dry out for about 4 hours after baking and before filling. This will crisp them up."

KEY TO PERFECTION

For meringues to be light and crisp, and not at all grainy, the egg whites should be beaten in two stages, and the superfine sugar should be added little by little to make sure that plenty of air is beaten in.

Before starting to beat, wipe around the inside of the bowl with the cut side of a lemon wedge. This will ensure that the bowl is clean and free of grease—essential for the egg whites to stiffen when whisked.

Beat the egg whites on their own to the soft peak stage. They should be floppy, and still quite wet.

Add the sugar to the partially beaten egg whites a heaped large spoonful at a time, beating for a minute after each addition. When all of the sugar has been added, the meringue should be glossy and stand in stiff peaks when the beater is lifted out.

ALL IS NOT LOST

If you break the meringues when you lift them off the sheet, or if you have any left over, you can make them into Eton Mess. Crumble them roughly into a bowl, then fold in whipped cream and crushed strawberries (the amounts of these are up to you). Serve within 1–2 hours, otherwise the meringues will lose their crispness.

"I have a range cooker so I can fit all the meringues on one very wide oven tray. This saves having to swap baking sheets halfway through cooking."

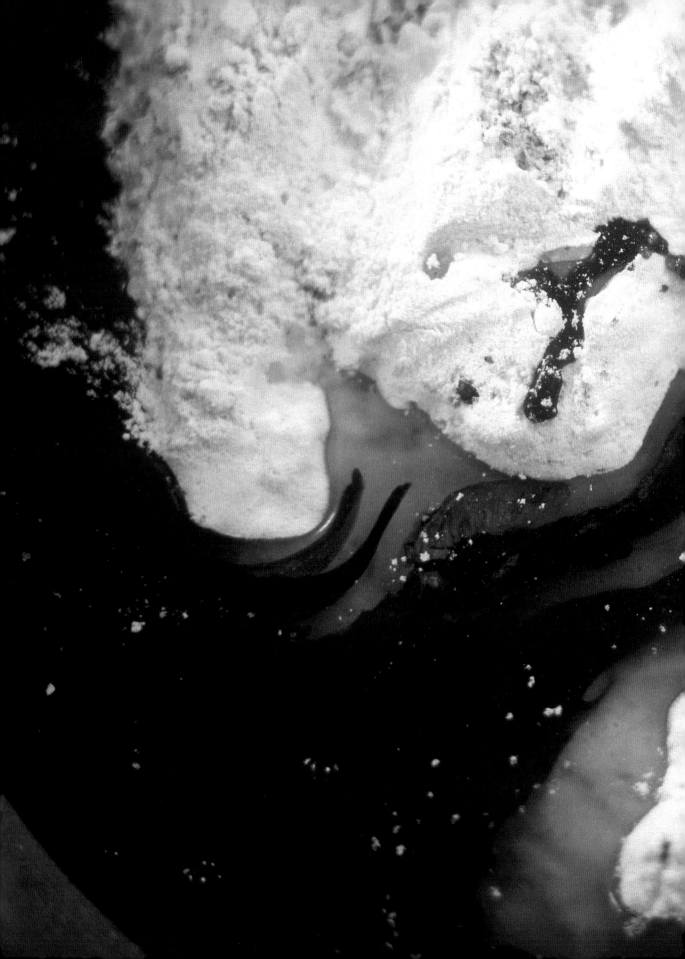

BAKING

BANANA BREAD

We always have bananas in the fruit bowl, because Jake and Archie are just crazy about them. If any bananas turn too soft to eat, we use them in a banana bread. This recipe is incredibly quick and simple.

CUTS INTO 10–12 SLICES
2 large eggs, preferably organic
1 tsp vanilla extract
1 tsp almond extract
2 cups all-purpose flour
1 tsp baking powder
$^{1}/_{4}$ tsp fine table salt
8 tbsp (1 stick) softened unsalted butter, plus extra for the pan
$^{1}/_{2}$ cup granulated sugar
4–5 large, overripe bananas, about 1$^{1}/_{2}$lb (550g) total weight, peeled and mashed
1 cup chopped walnuts

Preheat the oven to 375°F (190°C). Brush an 8$^{1}/_{2}$ x 4$^{1}/_{2}$ x 2$^{1}/_{2}$in (21 x 11 x 6cm) loaf pan with softened butter and line the bottom with waxed paper.

Beat the eggs in a bowl with the vanilla and almond extracts. Sift the flour into another bowl with the baking powder and salt.

Cream the butter and sugar together until light and fluffy, using the paddle attachment of an electric mixer on high speed. With the machine at low speed, slowly pour in the eggs, beating until they are completely incorporated (don't worry if the mix looks curdled at this point, as it will come together later). Turn the machine off.

Mix in the mashed bananas, then fold in the sifted dry ingredients and the walnuts, just until the ingredients come together. Pour into the loaf pan and place on a baking sheet. Bake in the top third of the oven for 55 minutes until firm to the touch but slightly moist in the center.

Cool in the pan for about 15 minutes, then turn out onto a wire rack and peel off the paper. Turn right side up and cool before slicing.

"If you have black or spotty, overripe bananas and no time to make this bread, put the bananas in the freezer. They will keep for months, and you can also use them to make great smoothies."

KEY TO PERFECTION

Well-ripened bananas with soft flesh and well-spotted skins just turning to black are essential for this bread to taste good and have a moist texture. Don't try to make it with underripe or yellow bananas, because they won't mash, mix, or bake well, and be careful not to overcook the bread or you will make it dry.

To test if the bread is done, insert a skewer in the center. With most cake batters the skewer should come out clean, but a perfectly cooked banana bread will have some moist crumbs clinging to it.

Mash the bananas with a fork until they're a loose, creamy consistency that will blend well with the other ingredients. This will be easy to do if the bananas are overripe because they'll offer no resistance. From 1½lb (550g) bananas, you'll get about 2 cups mashed flesh.

IRISH SODA BREAD

The best soda bread I've ever eaten is served at Bentley's, Richard Corrigan's restaurant in London. This is my version, and it's great cut in thick chunks, spread with plenty of unsalted butter.

MAKES 2 LOAVES
2/3 cups whole wheat flour, plus extra for dusting
2/3 cups self-rising flour
1 tbsp baking soda
1/2 cup rolled (old-fashioned) oats
3/4 cup wheat bran
1/2 cup wheat germ
1 1/4 tsp fine table salt
1/3 cup honey
1 1/2 tbsp unsulfured molasses
1 cup buttermilk

Preheat the oven to 350°F (180°C). Line a large baking sheet with parchment paper and dust with flour.

Put all the dry ingredients in a large bowl. Add the honey, molasses, and buttermilk, and mix together with your hands until you have a soft dough.

Turn the dough out onto a floured surface and divide in half with floured hands. Shape each half into a ball. Place on the baking sheet and flatten slightly.

Bake in the middle of the oven for 30 minutes until the breads sound hollow when they are tapped on the base. Cool on a wire rack.

KEY TO PERFECTION

Breads made with yeast must be kneaded well to develop the gluten in the flour or they won't rise. Soda bread has no yeast, so it requires hardly any work. In fact, you should handle the dough as little as possible—and the faster you mix the better.

When there are leaveners like baking soda and baking powder (in self-rising flour) in a dough, they are activated as soon as liquid is added. Work fast, mixing the ingredients lightly and quickly with your hands.

As soon as the dough starts to come together as a rough mass, stop mixing and take it out of the bowl. Never overmix this type of dough or the leaveners will exhaust themselves.

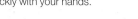

Shape the dough roughly—there's no need for a pan—and get it into the oven without delay. That's the beauty of soda bread—you don't have to wait for it to rise before baking.

BUTTER SHORTBREAD

When I make this deliciously rich shortbread at home, I simply cut it into chunky pieces, but in the restaurant I make slim, dainty shortbread fingers—you can see them with the Earl Grey Tea Cream on page 171. You can cut the shortbread into any shape you like.

MAKES ABOUT 20 PIECES
1¹/₃ cups all-purpose flour
pinch of fine table salt
¹/₃ cup white rice flour
¹/₂ cup superfine sugar,
   plus extra for dusting
1 cup (2 sticks) unsalted butter,
   frozen (you will use
   12 tbsp/1¹/₂ sticks)

Sift the flour and salt into a bowl and stir in the rice flour and sugar. Grate in 1¹/₂ sticks of the butter, then work it quickly into the flour until the mixture resembles fine bread crumbs.

Press the mix into an 8in (20cm) square baking pan and level the top. Refrigerate for about 1 hour.

Preheat the oven to 325°F (160°C).

Bake the shortbread for 35–40 minutes until light golden. Remove from the oven and prick all over with a fork, then mark into 20 pieces, cutting right through to the bottom of the pan. Dust liberally with sugar, then leave to cool before removing from the pan.

KEY TO PERFECTION

For buttery, melt-in-the-mouth shortbread, you need to work lightly and quickly. The less you handle the ingredients during mixing, the better.

Grate 12 tbsp (1¹/₂ sticks) of the butter into the flour mixture. By grating the butter, you hardly have to touch it, and the warmth of your hands won't have time to soften it.

Mix the butter into the flour by rolling the two together lightly between the palms of your hands. As the butter is grated into tiny pieces, the work's virtually done for you.

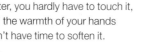

CHOCOLATE CAKE

In my mind this is the best chocolate cake ever—two moist layers filled and topped with a rich buttercream frosting and decorated with a ring of sliced almonds. It's a real family recipe, having been passed down through three generations, and we're happy to keep the tradition going.

SERVES 8–10
1²/₃ cups self-rising flour
¼ cup unsweetened cocoa
    powder
pinch of fine table salt
1 cup (2 sticks) softened
    unsalted butter, plus
    extra for the pans
1¼ cups granulated sugar
4 large eggs, preferably
    organic, beaten

TO FINISH
1½ cups confectioners' sugar
4 tbsp unsweetened cocoa
    powder
7 tbsp (½ stick plus 3 tbsp)
    softened unsalted butter
about 1 tbsp milk
a handful of sliced natural
    almonds

Preheat the oven to 350°F (180°C). Brush two 8 x 1in (20 x 2.5cm) round cake pans with softened butter and line the bottom and sides with waxed or parchment paper. Sift the flour, cocoa powder, and salt into a bowl. Set aside.

Cream the butter with the sugar until light and fluffy, using the paddle attachment of an electric mixer on high speed. Turn the speed down to low, then add the eggs a little at a time. Turn the machine off. Using a rubber spatula or a large metal spoon, fold in the flour and cocoa mixture one-third at a time until evenly incorporated.

Divide the batter equally between the pans and smooth the tops. Place in the center of the oven (preferably on the same shelf) and bake for 25 minutes. The cakes are done when a wooden skewer inserted in the center comes out clean. Leave to cool in the pans for 10 minutes, then unmold onto a wire rack and peel off the paper. Turn right side up and leave to cool completely.

To finish the cake, sift the confectioners' sugar and 2 tbsp of the cocoa powder into a bowl and beat in the butter to make a smooth, fluffy buttercream frosting. Sandwich the cakes together with two-thirds of the frosting. Sift the remaining cocoa powder into the rest of the frosting and soften with a little milk to make a spreading consistency. Spread on top of the cake, then sprinkle the almonds around the edge.

KEY TO PERFECTION

This dreamy chocolate cake is made by the creaming method. There are two important stages for success—the first one puts air into the mixture and the second keeps it there.

Fold the flour and cocoa into the creamed mixture using a figure eight motion. Folding is a technique that helps keep air in the mixture so the cakes will rise during baking and be light to eat. If you beat or stir, you'll knock out the air, the cakes won't rise well, and they'll be heavy.

Cream the butter and sugar together at high speed until pale in color and fluffy in texture. This will take 5–10 minutes, and the mixture should look white, almost like whipped cream. For the cake to rise and have a light, airy texture, correct creaming is essential.

ALL IS NOT LOST

If the mix starts to look curdled when you're adding the eggs, beat in a couple of spoonfuls of the flour and cocoa. This will halt the curdling immediately, then you can continue adding the rest of the eggs.

PINEAPPLE UPSIDE-DOWN CAKE

This was the very first thing I made in home economics class at school, and I remember taking it home on my bike to show my mother. It's really easy since it uses syrup from a can for the caramel. Later, when I was in college, my pastry teacher said I had a natural ability for baking, and for a while I did think about taking it up professionally. But I don't have any regrets—the heat of the kitchen is the place for me.

SERVES 8

2 cups self-rising flour
pinch of fine table salt
about 3–4 tbsp warmed golden
   syrup, plus extra for brushing
8 rings of canned pineapple
   (in syrup or natural juice),
   drained
11 candied cherries
1¼ cups (2½ sticks) softened
   unsalted butter, plus
   extra for the pan
1½ cups granulated sugar
5 large eggs, preferably organic,
   lightly beaten

Preheat the oven to 350°F (180°C). Sift the flour and salt into a bowl and set aside.

Butter an 11½ x 8½in (28.5 x 21cm) baking pan or dish. Line the bottom of the pan with parchment paper and brush with butter. Pour in the warm golden syrup. With the back of a spoon, spread the syrup evenly over the paper. Arrange the pineapple rings on the syrup in two rows of four, then place candied cherries in the center of the rings and in between.

Cream the butter and sugar together until light and fluffy, using the paddle attachment of an electric mixer on high speed. With the machine on low speed, slowly mix in the eggs. Turn the machine off. Using a rubber spatula or large metal spoon, fold the flour into the creamed mixture one-third at a time until completely incorporated.

Slowly pour the cake batter over the fruit in the pan, then spread the batter smooth so that it covers the fruit completely. Bake in the middle of the oven for 45 minutes until a skewer inserted in the center of the cake comes out clean. Leave the cake to cool in the pan on a wire rack for 5 minutes.

Run a sharp knife around the top edges of the cake to release it from the pan. Place a sheet of waxed or parchment paper on a wire rack, then unmold the cake onto the paper. Carefully peel away the lining paper, taking care not to tug on it and dislodge the fruit.

Brush enough warmed golden syrup over the cake to cover it liberally, then leave for a couple of minutes to let the syrup soak in. Serve the cake warm for dessert with custard sauce or cream, or cooled as a snacking cake (it will keep well for up to a week in an airtight container).

KEY TO PERFECTION

To look its best, this cake needs attention to detail when preparing the pan and arranging the fruit in the bottom.
If you take time at this stage, your efforts will be rewarded when you unmold the cake and get a perfect-looking result.

Taking care not to dislodge the pattern, pour and spoon the cake batter slowly in a line down each row of fruit. When all the fruit is covered, smooth over the top of the cake batter lightly with the back of the spoon.

Pour warm, runny syrup over the softened butter on the paper, then spread it out to a thick, even layer with the back of a spoon. This will hold the fruit in place and help make the cake nice and moist.

ENJOY COOKING

*"Last but not least, relax and be confident.
The food will taste all the better for it."*

SCONES WITH GOLDEN RAISINS

Before I married Jane we used to go to her house when we were dating, and her mom, Doreen, always had a freshly baked batch of pastries, cakes, or scones to offer. I could never resist—it was the best way to win a young man over.

MAKES 12–15

3 cups self-rising flour
1/2 tsp baking powder
pinch of fine table salt
7 tbsp (1/2 stick plus 3 tbsp)
    cold unsalted butter, diced
1/3 cup plus 1 tbsp granulated
    sugar
2/3 cup golden raisins
1 cup whole milk
1 large egg, preferably
    organic, beaten

Preheat the oven to 425°F (220°C). Line a baking sheet with parchment paper.

Sift the flour, baking powder, and salt into a bowl. Rub in the butter until the mixture resembles bread crumbs, loosely gathering the mixture together in your hands without squeezing or pressing. Stir in the sugar and raisins.

Mix the milk and egg together, then slowly pour two-thirds into the flour, stirring constantly with a table knife until the dough comes together. It should be quite firm, but moist, so add a little more of the milk mixture if it appears too dry.

Turn the dough onto a lightly floured surface and knead briefly for only a minute or two—just long enough to be able to shape it into a rough, loose ball. Now roll it out until it's about 3/4in (2cm) thick. Cut out scones using a 2 1/2in (6.5cm) round cookie cutter, dipping it in flour before each cut. Gather up the trimmings, knead very briefly until the dough comes together, and roll and cut out more scones.

Place the scones on the baking sheet and brush the tops lightly with the remaining milk mixture. Bake in the middle of the oven for 10–15 minutes until risen and light golden brown. Serve as soon as possible, preferably while still warm.

"When my mother-in-law comes to stay, she always makes these scones with the boys. They're such fun for children to make, and they turn out good to eat too."

KEY TO PERFECTION

Scones are very easy to make, but they need a light touch or they'll be chewy and stodgy, so work quickly and don't overhandle the dough.

Roll out the dough to ¾in (2cm) thickness on a lightly floured surface.
You can gather up the trimmings to cut out more scones, but don't roll the dough any thinner.

FLAPJACKS

These are not pancakes from the griddle, but bar cookies made with oats. Some people like flapjacks to be thick and soft, but I prefer them thinner and crunchier, so I've perfected my own recipe.

MAKES 12–16
2 cups rolled (old-fashioned) oats
1/2 cup raisins, chopped
pinch of fine table salt
10 tbsp (1 1/4 sticks) unsalted
   butter, plus softened butter
   for the pan
1/3 cup packed light brown sugar
4 tbsp golden syrup, plus
   a few extra spoonfuls
   warmed syrup for drizzling

Preheat the oven to 325°F fan (160°C). Brush a shallow 13 x 9in (33 x 23cm) baking pan with softened butter and line with parchment paper.

Mix the oats, raisins, and salt in a large bowl and make a well in the center. In a heavy pan, gently melt the butter with the sugar and syrup. Pour into the well, then gradually bring the oats into the center until everything is evenly combined.

With wet hands, press the mixture into the baking pan, making sure it goes right into the corners. Bake in the middle of the oven for 25 minutes. Remove from the oven and drizzle with syrup, then return to the oven to bake for 10 minutes longer until the edges are crisp.

Cut the flapjacks into squares while hot. Leave to cool in the pan, then remove and store in an airtight container.

KEY TO PERFECTION

To make crunchy flapjacks, you need surprisingly few ingredients. The secret lies in the way they are mixed and baked.

Use your hands to quickly combine the dry ingredients with the melted butter, syrup, and sugar. The mixture should be sticky, and come together easily when squeezed.

Toward the end of baking, drizzle warmed golden syrup over the flapjack mixture, then brush it in. This is how to make the inside gooey and the top sweet and crisp.

PETIT-BROWNIES

I like brownies to be pure gooey chocolate, with just a hint of crispness to bite through on the top. At the restaurant, we serve brownies in tiny squares as petits fours, but you can cut them larger to serve as a dessert with ice cream or whipped cream.

MAKES ABOUT 30
2 cups confectioners' sugar, plus extra for dusting
1 cup plus 2 tbsp all-purpose flour
⅓ cup plus 2 tbsp unsweetened cocoa powder
11oz (300g) high-quality bittersweet chocolate (at least 70% cocoa solids), chopped
13 tbsp (1½ sticks plus 1 tbsp) unsalted butter, diced, plus extra softened butter for the pan
4 tbsp golden syrup or corn syrup
4 large eggs, preferably organic, beaten
1 tbsp vanilla extract

Preheat the oven to 375°F (190°C). Brush a 13 x 9in (33 x 23cm) baking pan with softened butter and line the bottom and sides with parchment paper.

Mix the confectioners' sugar, flour, and cocoa powder in a large bowl. Set aside.

Melt the chocolate in a *bain marie* (pages 190–191). Remove the bowl from the pan, add the butter and golden syrup, and stir until they are melted and evenly incorporated with the chocolate. Leave to cool to room temperature.

Beat the eggs and vanilla extract into the chocolate mixture, then add to the dry ingredients and beat again until smooth. Pour into the baking pan and smooth the top. Bake in the middle of the oven for 20–25 minutes until the top is slightly cracked and the center feels soft and still a little moist. Leave to cool in the pan set on a wire rack.

Unmold the cake onto the rack and remove the parchment. Trim the edges to make them straight, then cut the brownies into squares. Sift confectioners' sugar over the brownies before serving.

KEY TO PERFECTION

The secret of perfectly formed, moist brownies is in the presentation and timing. For brownies to look as good as they taste, you must pay attention to detail before baking, and take the brownies out of the oven as soon as they're done.

Undercooking is the key. To check if the brownies are done, insert the tip of a sharp knife in the center. The knife should come out with some moist crumbs clinging to it. Don't be tempted to put the brownies back in the oven.

Lay a sheet of plastic wrap over the uncooked batter and smooth the wrap out with your fingertips so there are no wrinkles or creases. Press it gently into the corners and along the sides, then carefully peel it off. The surface of the brownie batter will be perfectly flat.

CHOCOLATE CHIP COOKIES

We keep these in an airtight container in the refrigerator—I love cold chocolate. When I come home from work late, it's hard not to grab a cookie or two. I find them irresistible.

MAKES ABOUT 20
1¼ cups all-purpose flour
½ tsp baking powder
pinch of fine table salt
8 tbsp (1 stick) softened unsalted butter
⅓ cup granulated sugar
⅓ cup packed light brown sugar
1 large egg, preferably organic, beaten
½ tsp vanilla extract
1 cup semisweet chocolate chips or chopped bittersweet chocolate

Sift the flour into a bowl with the baking powder and salt.

Cream the butter and both sugars together until light and fluffy, using the paddle attachment of an electric mixer on high speed. Turn the speed down to low and slowly mix in the egg. Add the vanilla extract. Turn the machine off. Using a rubber spatula, fold in the flour in two batches until evenly incorporated.

Fold the chocolate chips into the dough. Form into a log (about 10 x 2in/25 x 5cm) on a lightly floured surface and wrap in plastic wrap. Refrigerate for at least 2 hours until firm.

Preheat the oven to 350°F (180°C). Line a baking sheet with parchment paper.

Cut the chilled dough into about 20 slices, each about ½in (1cm) thick, and place them well apart on the baking sheet. Bake in the middle of the oven for 12–15 minutes until golden brown. Cool the cookies on the baking sheet, then keep in an airtight container.

"The cookie dough can be stored in the refrigerator for up to a week, so you can slice off and bake as many cookies as you like, when you like."

KEY TO PERFECTION

The dough must be well chilled or the cookies will spread out of shape during baking. Chilling also keeps the chocolate chips firm, so they remain chunky.

After shaping, wrap the log of dough tightly in a double layer of plastic wrap, then refrigerate to firm it up.

When you're ready to bake, slice off as many cookies as you want—the chilled dough will cut cleanly and neatly into disks.

Space the cookies well apart on the parchment-lined baking sheet so the heat can circulate freely around them. This will also ensure that they won't spread into each other.

BLUEBERRY MUFFINS

The muffins you see in the shops look the way they do because the pans are filled with too much batter. I don't think it's necessary to make them so huge. Why would you want to eat that much for breakfast anyway? Mine are smaller and perfectly formed.

MAKES 12
3 cups all-purpose flour
2 tsp baking powder
1 tsp fine table salt
3/4 tsp ground cinnamon
3/4 cup plus 2 tbsp granulated
   sugar
6 tbsp (3/4 stick) unsalted butter
1 cup whole milk
3 large eggs, preferably
   organic
1 cup fresh or frozen
   blueberries

Preheat the oven to 400°F (200°C). Line a standard-size muffin pan with paper cups.

Sift the flour into a large bowl with the baking powder, salt, and cinnamon. Stir in the sugar. Mix in the butter using a fork or pastry blender until the mixture resembles bread crumbs.

Using a fork, whisk together the milk and eggs. Whisk this liquid quickly into the flour mixture, then gently fold in the blueberries with a rubber spatula.

Divide the batter equally among the muffin cups. Bake the muffins in the middle of the oven for 20–25 minutes until risen and golden brown. Let cool in the pan for a few minutes before removing. Serve warm, or as soon as possible after baking.

KEY TO PERFECTION

For light-as-air muffins, you must mix quickly and lightly. This is especially important when making fruit muffins since there's more mixing involved.

After whisking the liquid into the dry ingredients, gently fold the blueberries through the batter using a spatula. Do this as quickly as possible, and don't try to make the batter smooth. It should be sloppy and lumpy.

INDEX

ACKNOWLEDGMENTS

Marcus Wareing would like to thank…

I am indebted to many people who have helped me with this book, but in particular I would like to thank my wife, Jane, for her love and support, and my young sons, Jake and Archie, who seem to be expressing a desire for cooking—or the camera. I'm not sure which.

I would also like to thank my chefs—Alyn Williams for his help in getting the recipes together, and Darren Velvick for assisting me on the photo shoots. A personal thank you, too, to all the team at Pétrus, who run the restaurant so smoothly when I'm not there, especially Jean-Philippe at the front and Tristan in the kitchen. And thank you Gordon, Chris, and Holdings, for your support, and Jo and Nicky at Sauce Communications.

Special thanks are also due to Mary-Clare Jerram at Dorling Kindersley, for giving me the opportunity to express myself on the page; to photographer David Loftus for making the food look so good; to Alex, Emma, and Saskia at Smith & Gilmour, whose art direction, styling, and design have made the book stunning; and to Rosie Scott and Abbie Kornstein for assisting on the photo shoots. I would also like to say how grateful I am to Angela Nilsen, who meticulously tested every recipe.

Last but by no means least, a massive thank you to my co-author, Jeni Wright, for her patience and skill in helping me write my first book. Her attention to detail and relentless quest for perfection have been amazing. She has driven me insane—but the end result is worth it.

Dorling Kindersley would like to thank…

Norma MacMillan for her outstanding editorial skill and professionalism, Ariane Durkin for her excellent editorial assistance, Caroline de Souza for her invaluable design assistance, and Hilary Bird for producing the index.